The Intelligent Quality Growth Investor

2025 Edition

How To Invest In The World's Finest Companies

Written by Long Equity

What's new in the third edition?

The first edition of this book spanned 71 pages and was written in just six days over the 2022 Christmas break.

The second edition expanded significantly to 160 pages and was written over a few months in 2023.

The third edition, which you're now holding, is the result of a year's effort over the course of 2024 and comprises over 200 pages of updated insights and refined content.

So, what's new?

To begin with, two new chapters have been added: one on pricing power and another on business models. All data has been refreshed and the mental models have been expanded and clarified. Additionally, a wealth of new ideas have been introduced throughout the book.

This edition is packed with the latest market insights, equipping you with the knowledge to navigate 2025 with confidence.

Since the last edition, there's also now a data service. If you're interested in a frequently maintained list of quality growth companies and their quality growth metrics then visit: www.longeq.com

Contents

Prologue to the 2025 version

Every investor can learn something from Captain America.

Before becoming a superhero, Steve Rogers was brave, but weak. A dose of Super Soldier Serum made him grow, enhanced his strength and transformed him into a superhero. While Cap found his source of growth in serum, as investors we can find it in companies that can invest their capital at high returns.

It wasn't just anyone who could take on the Super Soldier Serum. Steve Rogers was chosen because of his courage and integrity. This was because the serum worked by amplifying not just physical traits, but also character, thus making good people better and bad people worse. In investing, debt has a similar function. Good companies use debt to become better companies, while for bad companies debt can magnify weaknesses and become highly destructive.

Shortly after becoming Captain America, the Super Soldier Serum was destroyed and its formula lost. There could only be one Cap. The best businesses are also irreproducible. They have unique traits that give them pricing power and that other companies find impossible to copy. In investing, we should look for businesses that can't be replicated.

Not only was Captain America filled with serum, he was also given a shield made from an indestructible metal called vibranium. It could withstand anything that was thrown at it. Investors need to look for companies that can also withstand anything that's thrown at it. Whether that's threats from competitors or economic cycles. Businesses become supercharged when there are barriers to competition and resilience to economic threats.

Having served in World War 2, Cap found himself in the icy waters of the North Atlantic. Presumed dead, he became frozen into a block of ice. Decades later, in the modern day, he was discovered and thawed. Historically, many investors have benefitted by also putting their portfolio on ice - sitting back, doing nothing and waiting a few decades for their investments to compound in value.

Just like Captain America's journey, successful investing requires finding companies with strong foundations and irreplaceable qualities, and having the patience to let time reveal their potential.

Prologue to the 2024 version

Every investor should watch Pixar's short film Piper.

The story follows a flock of sandpipers fishing for crabs and clams. As each wave recedes, the invertebrates quickly bury back under the sand before the next wave approaches. Each wave provides only a short window of time for the sandpipers to locate their next meal before it disappears below the grains of sand.

Piper, the main character, is still a chick and finds herself struggling to catch the crabs and clams in time. If that wasn't enough, she's also fearful of the waves. Suddenly a wave catches Piper off guard, dragging her beneath the water. But rather than the ocean being as terrifying as she had imagined it to be, Piper finds herself enjoying life underwater.

From under the sea, she soon notices that each time a wave comes in, the clams briefly lift out from below the sand, before burying again. Now, each time the waves recede, Piper knows the exact location where they are hiding. This allows her to greatly increase the number she catches. Piper finds herself in a position to share what she catches with the other sandpipers that are not daring enough to go under the waves.

Here's the message for investors. In the film, Piper did three things. She changed her viewpoint to one not shared by the crowd. She used her new viewpoint to gain an information advantage. She then used her advantage to increase her success rate.

Having all the information matters.

My hope is that this book will help change how you view financial markets so you can find the investment opportunities others don't see.

Chapter 1:
Generating Investment Ideas

The investable universe

The investable universe has thousands of publicly listed companies for investors to choose from. Hidden in this universe are a small cluster of businesses that share several financial characteristics. They consistently generate high returns on their investments over long periods of time, they raise their prices without losing sales and they are resilient to competition and economic downturns. Investors in such "quality growth" companies have historically been rewarded with high share price appreciation.

Presented in this book are mental models for finding quality growth companies. Mental models are a thought process for turning complex information quickly and accurately into actionable insights. They allow for investors to filter out the noise and to separate what's important from what's not.

If you're researching a company and you see that it's just made $1 billion in profit, can you conclude that it's going to be a great investment opportunity? The answer is no, it's an impossible question to answer without context. You need something to compare that $1 billion in profit to.

First, you need to know the profits made in previous years, so you can determine whether the profits are growing and whether that growth is predictable or cyclical. Then you need to know how much capital the company invested to generate the profit. This reveals whether the company is making good returns on its investments. Then you need to know how much the company made in sales, in order to determine how much of its sales revenue it kept as profit. Lastly, you need to compare the company to other companies. This ensures you only invest in the best possible opportunities.

Not every quality company is growing and not every growing company has a quality business. The mental models presented in this book are focused on understanding a company's four most important attributes for deciding whether it is an investable quality growth company.

They are:

1. Growth,

2. Capital efficiency,

3. Pricing power, and

4. Valuation.

The mental models are based on four financial ratios centred around free cash flow (FCF):

1. **FCF per share growth** - for measuring growth,

2. **FCF return on capital** - for analysing capital efficiency,

3. **FCF margin** - for assessing pricing power, and

4. **FCF yield** - for determining valuation.

We will get to what free cash flow is, what these four ratios mean and how they can be calculated in the subsequent chapters.

The core skills of an investor

To invest in listed companies is to buy a percentage of a business trading on a financial market. Investors need to be able to differentiate between analysing a company and analysing a company's shares. These aren't the same, but are both essential.

Investors need to understand business, accountancy and corporate finance so they can analyse what's going on inside the companies they invest in. Investors also need to understand financial markets, economics and valuation so they can analyse what's influencing the share price of the companies they own. The aim of this book has been to condense all the core principles from these subjects into the pages you are reading now.

The chapters on growth and margins explore core accounting concepts, such as the income statement and free cash flow. The chapter on capital efficiency considers the three rules of corporate finance and looks at company balance sheets. The chapters on pricing power and business models consider the competitive advantages, barriers to entry and barriers to scale that create pricing power. The chapter on valuation considers principles from economics and financial markets to ensure investors avoid (or at least minimise) overpaying. And lastly, the chapter on portfolio construction considers principles from behavioural finance to understand how to construct and manage a portfolio prudently.

This book is designed to be read in 2-3 hours. In this chapter we will start by covering how to search the investable universes from multiple angles. You can use these techniques to create a shortlist of investment ideas for you to further research using the mental models in the chapters that follow. This will ensure only the best companies have your attention. Let's get started.

Screen for high quality growth companies

Stock screens are often the starting place used by investors to search for companies that have specific financial metrics. Typically these metrics are based around growth, profitability, balance sheet strength, margins and valuation. While this sounds helpful, stock screens can have shortfalls. Firstly, many stock screeners use generic financial metrics that appeal to a broad range of investors, such as revenue growth and price-to-earnings (P/E) ratios. They are less likely to offer the rarer and more insightful metrics presented in this book. Secondly, many stock screeners have a tendency to be focused on short-term metrics (e.g. growth over the last year or quarter) and aren't suited for looking at long-term trends (e.g. average returns and growth rates over the last 10+ years).

Thirdly and most importantly, many of the advantages that the world's best companies have are often subtle and can't be detected using screens, such as intangible advantages, like pricing power and switching costs. Screening for companies with high earnings growth, high returns on capital, high margins and low debt reduces the number of companies to be researched, but it only gets you part of the way there. Investors looking for an edge over other investors need to do things differently.

Analyse supply chains

Investors can create an edge for themselves by developing an in-depth knowledge of multiple supply chains.

Every business has suppliers and customers. These relationships come together to create a complex global web of supply chains. Some companies produce raw materials, others transform these materials into component parts, while others assemble the components into a finished product that are sold to end users: either individual consumers or companies. Alongside each supply chain you have the companies that provide the equipment and services that make it all possible.

When researching a company an investor should study its suppliers and customers to help understand where in the chain that the majority of the value is being created. More often than not this will reveal the most attractive investment ideas.

Set out below are high level summaries of several supply chains:

- Coca Cola buys sugar (the second largest ingredient in Coke after water) and flavourings from a range of suppliers worldwide. They then supply their beverages to retailers and restaurants, including McDonalds, where they are then sold directly to consumers.

- Consumer staple companies, like Nestle and Procter & Gamble, buy raw agricultural products (e.g. cocoa, coffee, milk), chemicals (e.g. fragrances, surfactants and dyes) and packaging from a range of suppliers, which are then used in the creation of their products. They then supply their products to retailers, such as Walmart and Costco, where they are then sold directly to consumers in their stores.

- The credit score company Fair Isaac (also known as FICO) buys credit data from the three major credit bureaus, Experian, Equifax and TransUnion. These three credit bureaus also have their own suppliers. Fair Isaac uses the data to create credit scores, which it then sells to many of the world's banks, insurers, credit card companies and retailers.

- The semiconductor supply chain is an example of a complex supply chain filled with high quality companies. The supply chain includes the designers of chips (e.g. AMD, Intel and NVIDIA), the manufacturers of chips (e.g. TSMC), the creators of the equipment and software needed to design and manufacture chips (e.g. Applied Materials, ASML and Cadence Design Systems) and the consumers of chips (e.g. the manufacturers of electronic equipment, such as computers and smartphones). Even the creators of semiconductor equipment, like Applied Materials and ASML, have their own supply chains for all the parts that go into their machines. It's one of the world's most complex supply chains, both in terms of the number of countries and continents involved, but also the number of companies, many of which operate in niches where they are the monopoly.

- In creating its iPhone, Apple buys semiconductors manufactured by TSMC, speciality glass from Corning and the assembly services of Foxconn. It then sells its iPhones directly to retail consumers, enterprise customers and large telecoms companies, like Verizon and AT&T, who bulk purchase smartphones for resale.

- In building their aeroplanes, Boeing purchases aerospace components from Honeywell, flight control systems from Rockwell Collins and jet engines from GE Aerospace. Boeing then sells its aircraft to airlines (like Delta Air Lines and American Airlines), as well as to government, the military and leasing companies.

In depth analysis into supply chains often unearths a wide range of companies to research further. But analysis of a supply chain isn't complete without also considering the competitors engaging with those supply chains.

Analyse the competition

Companies compete with other companies.

They can compete when buying supplies from suppliers, and they can compete when selling similar products and services to the same market.

Companies compete on quality (i.e. offering a similar or superior product to their competitor), on price (i.e. offering a lower price to their competitor) and on customer service (i.e. providing a more convenient purchasing experience).

Some companies, like airlines and banks, operate in sectors filled with large numbers of competitors all vying for market share. Other sectors are far less concentrated with competitors.

Markets filled with competing companies benefit buyers, giving them a variety of options to choose from. To succeed, companies in saturated markets are forced to compete on price and spend significantly on marketing. In contrast, markets dominated by only a few companies offer buyers little choice. As differentiating themselves from competitors isn't necessary, such companies don't need to offer a competitive price and don't need to spend large sums on marketing, which can lead to long-term profitability.

Investment ideas can be generated by looking for companies where there are low levels of competition and then considering the companies that are directly competing with each other in that market.

A monopoly is where there is a single seller of a particular product or service within a given industry or geography. This means they have complete control of the price and the level of supply of the product they sell.

Examples of monopolies:

- Airports - there's typically only one airport per city.

- Alphabet - has a dominant position across several digital markets, especially in online search (Google).

- ASML - has a dominant player in advanced photolithography machines for semiconductor manufacturing.

- EssilorLuxottica - has a dominant position in lens manufacturing and eyewear retail.

- Fair Isaac (FICO) - has a dominant position in methodologies for credit scoring and the acceptance of their scores across the financial sector.

- Stock exchanges - there's typically a dominant exchange per major market.

- TSMC - has a dominant position in production of cutting-edge semiconductors.

- Verisign - effectively holds a monopoly for top-level website domains.

A duopoly is where two companies dominate a particular market together. There are many examples of duopolies that provide similar products and services in the same market. While they can compete directly for the same clients, often their coexistence strengthens the other by forcing innovation and efficiency. Like a monopoly, duopolies can enjoy high barriers to entry. As an investor you can treat duopolies as a monopoly, by buying both for your portfolio. Set out below is a list of duopolies that enjoy strong market positions and are worth researching further. Some will be familiar and some perhaps less so.

Examples of duopolies:

- Boeing and Airbus - dominant in aerospace.

- Cadence Design Systems and Synopsys - dominant in semiconductor design software.

- Coca Cola and PepsiCo - dominant in soft drinks.

- Fisher & Paykel Healthcare and ResMed - dominant in healthcare for respiratory disease.

- IDEXX and Zoetis - dominant in veterinary testing and diagnostics.

- L'Oreal and Estee Lauder - dominant in cosmetics.

- McDonald's and Burger King - dominant in fast food.

- Microsoft and Apple - dominant in operating systems.

- Nike and Adidas - dominant in sports apparel.

- S&P Global and Moody's - both credit rating agencies are dominant in credit rating.

- Sonova and Cochlear - dominant in technology for hearing loss.

- Visa and MasterCard - dominant in credit card payments.

Investment ideas can also be generated by looking for similar companies in different markets. Such companies may have a monopoly or duopoly regionally, but not worldwide. For example, the largest e-commerce business in North America is Amazon.com. If you decide that you like the e-commerce business model, you may choose to look for similar e-commerce opportunities in other countries such as JD.com, the largest e-commerce company in China, and Mercado Libre, the largest e-commerce company in Central and South America.

Find what's worked in the past

There's a general consensus in the investing world, and in other fields such as sport, that winners keep on winning. This is often due to a combination of factors, such as competitive strength and management's focus on the long-term. While it is impossible to directly screen for stocks with these qualitative properties, we can indirectly screen for them by looking for companies that have managed to grow consistently over long periods of time.

The following table sets out a list of US companies that experienced the highest share price growth rates over both a 30 and 40 year time period (1984-2024 and 1994-2024 respectively). For example, the table shows that Danaher grew its share price at an annualised rate of 20.9% a year over 4 decades and 17.3% a year over 3 decades. Each of the companies listed below have therefore created massive amounts of value for their shareholders. Qualitative research into each of these companies reveals a history of diligent capital allocation and the creation of defensive shields to fend off competition.

Company	40yr CAGR	Company	30yr CAGR
Monster Beverage	30.2%	UnitedHealth	23.5%
NVR, Inc.	28.4%	Amgen	22.4%
Apple	24.3%	Apple	21.1%
O'Reilly Auto Parts	22.1%	Danaher	20.9%
Ross Stores	21.8%	Home Depot	20.0%
Fair Isaac	21.8%	Stryker	19.4%
Old Dominion	21.1%	Applied Materials	18.8%
Amphenol	19.3%	Paychex	18.7%
Tractor Supply	19.2%	Expeditors Intl	18.0%
Costco	17.6%	Nike	17.6%
Adobe	17.4%	Cintas	17.4%
Danaher	17.3%	Jacobs Solutions	16.3%
Intuit	17.2%	Lam Research	16.2%
Cooper Companies	17.1%	Lowe's	15.8%
IDEXX Laboratories	16.9%	Sherwin-Williams	15.6%
Microsoft	16.9%	Aflac	15.1%
Jack Henry	16.7%	Thermo Fisher	14.9%
UnitedHealth	16.6%	W. R. Berkley Corp	14.8%
Oracle Corporation	16.4%	Trane Technologies	14.7%
Expeditors Intl	16.2%	Lennar	14.7%
Stryker	16.1%	Walmart	14.3%
Roper Technologies	16.0%	Caterpillar Inc.	14.3%
Qualcomm	15.7%	Medtronic	14.2%
Sherwin-Williams	15.7%	Costco	14.2%

No doubt a lot of these names will be familiar to you. But what may surprise you is that a lot of these companies are somewhat mundane. There's evidently a lot of money to be made in paint (Sherwin-Williams), energy drinks (Monster), athletic clothing (Nike) and retail (Costco, Home Depot).

Such CAGR tables are fairly easy to put together. All you need is a spreadsheet that can pull financial data. Next you will need to find a list of companies and their stock tickers. I suggest starting with the S&P 500 (the 500 largest publicly traded US companies), before moving on to non-US indices and small/mid cap indices. It's then just a case of pulling the current share price, the historic share price (e.g. 10, 20 or 30 years ago) and then calculating the compound average growth rate (CAGR), which is the average growth rate per year. The CAGR equation is set out below. Simply input the starting and ending share price and replace "n" with the number of years between the two share prices.

$$CAGR = [(End\ Value\ /\ Start\ Value) \wedge (1\ /\ n) - 1] * 100\%$$

Use regression to find consistent and incremental share price growth

A particularly helpful enhancement to the preceding method is the introduction of linear or exponential regression. Don't be put off by these mathematical terms, they are incredibly easy to get your head around.

In investing, returns can either be consistent or erratic. Knowing that a company grew its share price by 100% over the last 5 years doesn't tell you whether its growth was incremental or occurred rapidly in a short burst.

Over the last 15 years (2009-2024) Texas Instruments (the semiconductor company) and Incyte (the pharmaceutical company) both generated an annualised share price return of 15% each year. Where they differ is the linearity of their share price growth. Linearity simply refers to how straight a line is. It is measured using something called R-Squared (RSq). A perfectly straight line that's going up has an RSq of 1.00 and a perfectly straight line that's going down has a RSq of -1.00. When looking at the linearity of share prices, ideally a RSq value above 0.85 over a 10+ year time period implies consistent share price appreciation.

Texas Instruments had a 15 year share price RSq of 0.95, while Incyte was 0.48. If we compare their share price charts we see what this means.

Between 2009-2024 Texas Instrument's share price grew consistently and predictably:

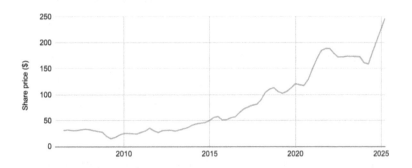

While Incyte's growth was significantly more cyclical:

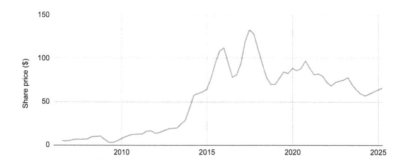

Texas Instruments represents a class of companies often referred to as compounders. They have a long history of being profitable, reinvesting their profits and not being overly impacted by economic downturns. Incyte represents companies that are more cyclical. Such companies are often exposed to economic and business cycles, such as interest rates, employment and commodity prices. While both classes of companies provide opportunities for making money, the focus of this book is very much compounders, that have high quality underlying businesses, as they lend themselves to less volatile and more predictable investing.

While most data from the financial markets is noisy and meaningless, screening for linear and exponential growth unearths companies that have incrementally increased their share price over long time periods. It's not possible to achieve consistent share price growth without also having consistent earnings growth.

High linearity in particular means low volatility, which implies that these high quality businesses have high quality shareholders. High quality shareholders are shareholders that invest and hold for the long-term. They do this because they are patient and appreciate that compounding takes time. Companies mostly owned by high quality shareholders do not see their share price subjected to wild swings in trading volumes and shorting. Linearity is a powerful reverse-engineering method for finding companies that have low share price volatility and are therefore likely to be owned by high quality shareholders.

Calculating linearity is a fairly straightforward and fast method for screening for high quality companies. Again, it requires a spreadsheet capable of pulling financial data. You will need share price data at 6 month intervals starting from the current date going back ideally 10 years or more. The correlation function in your spreadsheet will be able to calculate the linearity for you. You then use the correlation function to compare the time series (x-axis) with the share price (y-axis). You can then use the following formula in your spreadsheet:

$$= CORREL(x\text{-}axis, y\text{-}axis)$$

To help get you started the following table sets out the US companies that from 2009-2024 compounded their share price over 15% per year with a linearity greater than 0.95. Analysis of the underlying business of companies that have experienced linear share price growth typically reveals consistent earnings growth and is therefore a useful reverse engineering technique for identifying high quality companies.

Company	15yr CAGR	15yr Linearity
Mastercard	23%	0.96
Ulta Beauty	23%	0.95
UnitedHealth	22%	0.96
Monster Beverage	22%	0.98
S&P Global	21%	0.95
Visa	20%	0.97
Rollins, Inc.	19%	0.97
Constellation Brands	19%	0.97
Teledyne Technologies	19%	0.96
Ross Stores	19%	0.96
Cooper Companies	18%	0.97
Ametek	18%	0.95
Verisk	17%	0.96
Roper Technologies	17%	0.98
A. O. Smith	17%	0.95
Broadridge Financial	17%	0.96
Cigna	17%	0.97
Marsh McLennan	17%	0.95
Aon	16%	0.96
Equinix	16%	0.97
Nordson Corporation	16%	0.97
Electronic Arts	16%	0.98
Accenture	16%	0.96
Texas Instruments	15%	0.95

Borrow ideas from the world's best fund managers

While it's important to generate your own ideas, it's also helpful to keep a watchful eye on what other investors are up to, in order to check your blindspot.

Understanding how something works is a science. If you've ever broken something, just to see if you can put it back together, then you've dabbled in the world of reverse engineering. Reverse engineering is a powerful tool for figuring out what makes something tick. It involves taking something apart, inspecting all individual parts, and then attempting to reassemble what you've taken apart. The process should reveal both how and why something is constructed the way that it is.

Reverse engineering can be applied to investing. For investors starting out, a great exercise is to compile a list of several top performing funds. To understand what has driven their performance you can then analyse the companies that each fund holds. You will soon notice something quite interesting. The holdings of many top funds often overlap. This means there is often consensus among investors on what is worth investing in.

Today finding the companies that a fund holds is quite straightforward. Funds that hold US companies are required to file a publicly available report each quarter called a 13F. This sets out all of their US holdings, but excludes their non-US holdings. The international part of their portfolio can be deduced from other documents. Many funds publish monthly factsheets of their top 10 holdings and annual reports of their complete portfolio. These sources can be consolidated to elucidate the full picture.

To help get you started, the following table summarises where there is consensus and overlap between 11 leading global equity funds focused on high quality growth businesses. Over 6 of the funds screened held Alphabet, Mastercard, Microsoft, Moody's and Visa. Companies with less consensus (e.g. Fair Isaac and MSCI) can also be a useful source of investment ideas, as this suggests that they may have been overlooked by other investors. Funds often trade in and out of positions, so it's helpful to update the list 2 - 4 times a year, so that you always have a source of interesting companies to research. Note that this approach shouldn't be used to outsource your research to managers of large funds, rather it's just a helpful technique to increase your exposure to potentially interesting investment ideas.

3	4 - 6	≥7
Accenture	Moody's	Visa
ASML	S&P Global	Microsoft
Fair Isaac	Amazon	Alphabet
Meta Platforms	Cadence Design	Mastercard
MSCI	Intuit	
Verisk Analytics	Thermo Fisher	
Waters		
Zoetis		

Analysing your investment ideas

It's perhaps unsurprising that "enabling" companies are often at the top of lists of quality companies. A consumer turning on their computer is likely to have engaged with either an Apple or Microsoft product. They may then go online to search and buy something they need, and in doing so they are more than likely to have used Google and/or Amazon to find and buy what they're after. Finally, the payment of such a transaction is likely to have been facilitated by either Visa or Mastercard.

The techniques in this chapter can be used to create a list of companies to research further. Having generated investment ideas from these multiple angles, you can then move on to analysing the companies in more detail using the techniques discussed in the following chapters.

We will next consider three important ratios for studying the quality of a company: free cash flow per share (for growth), free cash flow margin (for value creation) and free cash flow return on capital (for capital efficiency). For each ratio we will consider how to calculate it, how to interpret it, the types of companies that excel and common pitfalls to avoid.

Chapter 2:
Free cash flow per share (Growth)

A mental model for understanding businesses

Having looked at how to find potential investments, we can now turn to evaluating these companies. The best place to start is to consider:

1. Whether they sell a **product** (e.g. smartphones) or a **service** (e.g. streaming subscriptions).

2. Whether they sell to **consumers** (e.g. household items sold by a retailer) or to **businesses** (e.g. industrial parts sold to manufacturers).

3. Whether they sell a **discretionary purchase** (e.g. new cars for consumers or marketing for businesses) or an **essential purchase** (e.g. toothpaste for consumers or cybersecurity for businesses).

4. Whether what is being sold is a **recurring sale** (e.g. consumables and subscriptions) or a **one-off sale** (e.g. manufacturing equipment).

5. Whether what they are selling is a **major expense** for the buyer (e.g. an airline buying a new aeroplane) or a **minor expense** for the buyer (e.g. low cost disposable surgical items).

6. Whether they have a **concentrated customer base** in that they are selling to a small number of customers in a single industry (e.g. there are three main buyers of semiconductor manufacturing equipment) or a **diversified customer base** in that they are selling to a wide range of customers across multiple industries (e.g. Microsoft Word and Excel are used by a large number of businesses across all sectors).

7. Whether they sell to an **established market** (e.g. the supply and demand seen for skincare products has been around for millenia) or an **developing market** (e.g. the supply and demand seen for graphic processing units is fairly recent).

8. Whether they sell to a **single end-market** (e.g. Boeing services a single industry, aerospace) or **multiple end-markets** (e.g. 3M sells to multiple industries, including healthcare and construction).

The most resilient revenues are found in companies selling recurring, essential and affordable services to a diversified base of corporate clients. Software-as-a-service companies and payroll providers are great examples. Such businesses should be able to maintain long-term growth. The least resilient revenues are found in companies selling one-off, discretionary and expensive products directly to a small number of consumers or businesses. While profits can of course be created here, such companies are more likely to be exposed to economic downturns, shocks to their supply chain, threats from competition, and overall are more likely to struggle to grow.

Short-term (cyclical) vs long-term (secular) growth

A company's growth will be driven by either short-term or long-term trends.

Cyclical companies are exposed to short-term fluctuations tied to the business cycle and the economic cycle. Industries sensitive to these cycles include airlines, automotive companies, banks, construction companies, energy companies and companies selling discretionary goods. As these companies are buyers of raw materials and often rely on significant debt, their profitability is greatly impacted by the rise and fall of commodity prices and interest rates. They often experience high growth during economic expansion (particularly when consumer spending rises) and low growth or even losses during economic downturns and recessions (particularly when households look to cut costs). Consequently demand for discretionary items, such as new cars and overseas travel, declines during a downturn. Investors looking to benefit from cyclical growth require the ability - or to put it more accurately, the luck - to time the market and to predict when cycles start and finish.

In contrast to the short-term fluctuations of cyclical growth, secular growth refers to growth trends that persist over multiple years and decades. Rather than the short-term business and economic cycles, secular growth is driven by long-term trends, which are not strongly swayed by short-term cycles and are relatively insulated from economic shocks. This type of growth is often found in the technology, healthcare and consumer sectors, and fuels multi-decade growth in the stock market.

In the short-term, a cyclical company and a secular company may both be enjoying strong earnings growth and consequently share price growth. However, a cyclical company's growth is likely to eventually subside as the cycle completes, while a company benefiting from a long-term trend is more likely to enjoy growth for years or even decades into the future. Investors should favour companies benefiting from long-term trends, not short-term trends.

Current examples of long-term trends include:

- **Technological advancement** - Technology has been a driver of economic growth for decades, if not centuries. It has increased productivity across the global economy, which has been driven by automation and the rise in specialist technology. Current growth trends include AI, cloud computing and the rise in cybersecurity threats, and also the transition to electric vehicles.

- **Population growth and an ageing population** - The human population has been growing exponentially since the 1800s, although the growth rate is now slowing. At the same time urbanisation has seen more people move to cities, with now over half the world's population living in urban areas. The expansion of the middle class has fueled a rise in consumer discretionary spending, particularly in emerging economies. The trend towards longer lifespans has resulted in ageing populations. Together these trends are reshaping the labour market and providing a boost for healthcare and consumer companies, but they are also presenting challenges, particularly regarding pensions and the consumption of natural resources.

- **Structural changes to the economy** - Several structural shifts are transforming the global economy. This includes the move towards renewable energy and efforts to reduce dependency on fossil fuels. The globalisation of supply chains has fueled economic growth, but can also be vulnerable to trade tensions and geopolitical threats.

Once we understand the drivers of growth, we can better understand the growth seen on a company's financial statements.

The best financial metric for measuring growth

As investors we want our investments to grow, but exactly what part of a company should we be looking at for growth? The options include looking at a company's balance sheet to see whether its assets and equity are growing. Alternatively, you could go to the company's income statement to see whether its revenues and net income are growing, thus ensuring there's both top-line and bottom-line growth.

In this chapter we will consider the optimal metric for studying corporate growth. This will involve taking a journey. We will start with revenue, which is the money generated by a company when it sells its products and services. Along the way we will see how revenue becomes net income and how net income becomes free cash flow. We will then finish at one of the closest figures we can get to that reflects the earnings actually belonging to shareholders: free cash flow per share. As investors we need to look for top to bottom growth, which means ensuring that revenue and free cash flow per share are both growing.

Revenue

Revenue is the total amount of money generated from a company's sale of its products and services. This is the top line of a company's income statement.

Revenue is calculated by multiplying the volume of goods and services sold by their respective prices.

$$Volume \times Price = Revenue$$

This means that a business looking to maximise its revenue has only two options: it can either sell more or raise prices. Selling more requires a company to increase its market share in existing markets and to enter into new markets. Raising prices requires a company to have pricing power, which is the ability to raise prices, ideally above the rate of inflation, without seeing a significant decline in sales.

Revenue can be broken down into the proportion of revenue it generates from each product and service it sells or the revenue it generates from each geographic region it operates in. For example, Apple's revenue can be split either into sales of iPhones, iPads and MacBooks, and can also be split into sales across each continent. So when studying a company's growth, it's important to consider which products and geographies are driving the growth, and which are potentially acting as a headwind.

Gross profit

Producing the goods and services sold to generate revenues comes with costs. Cost of revenue (also known as cost of goods sold) represents the direct costs incurred in the production or acquisition of goods that a company sells, such as raw materials and labour. The figure reflects the expenses directly tied to the manufacturing or purchase of the goods and does not include other operational expenses such as sales, marketing, or administrative costs. Deducting the cost of revenue from the company's revenue gives the gross profit. Therefore, gross profit can be maximised by optimising the supply chain to keep the cost of producing the goods sold low.

Revenue - Cost of Revenue = Gross Profit

Operating profit

Companies also have operating expenses, such as sales and marketing (S&M) costs, general and administrative (G&A) costs, and research and development (R&D) costs. Additionally, there are non-cash expenses, known as depreciation and amortisation (D&A). Depreciation represents the depreciation in value of long-term tangible assets, such as machinery. Similarly, amortisation refers to the decrease in value over time of intangible assets, such as patents and other forms of intellectual property. Subtracting S&M, G&A, R&D and D&A (collectively known as the operating expenses, or OPEX) from gross profit gives the operating profit. Therefore, operating profit can be maximised by optimising the efficiency of a company's operations.

Gross Profit - Operating Expenses = Operating Profit

Net income

To get to the bottom line of a company's income statement we need to adjust for interest expense, which is the cost a company has to pay on its outstanding debts, and tax, which is the amount of profit owed by the company to the government. Subtracting interest expense and tax from a company's operating profit results in the net income.

Operating Profit - Interest Expense - Tax = Net Income

Minimising these last two expenses requires a company to be prudent with how and when it takes on debt, and to structure its business in a tax efficient manner.

The below Sankey diagram illustrates the journey from the top line to the bottom line of the income statement.

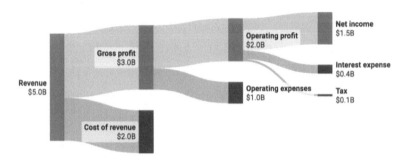

Having considered the income statement we can now draw an important conclusion. Companies looking to grow profits only have three options: sell more, raise prices and cut costs. Investors should therefore look for companies that:

- can grow market share and enter new markets - to **sell more**,

- have pricing power and flex it - to **raise prices**, and

- operate increasingly efficiently - to **cut costs**.

Operating cash flow

The problem with net income is that its calculation requires deducting the two non-cash expenses: depreciation and amortisation.

D&A are accounting techniques that can be used strategically in certain circumstances. One common example is when, instead of recognising a one-time expense on the income statement as a cash outflow, the accountant chooses to capitalise it instead. This means the expense is recorded on the balance sheet as an asset. The value of that created asset is then gradually reduced over time through depreciation or amortisation at a rate determined by the accountant. If a lower rate of devaluation than necessary is used, then this artificially inflates the value of the balance sheet, making the company appear more financially stable than it is. Additionally, manipulating D&A can create the illusion of smoother earnings over time, as lowering the rate that the asset devalues boosts operating profit and net income. As D&A are non-cash expenses, the calculation of operating cash flow brings them both back in, so that we have a clearer picture of the actual cash that has flowed in and out.

Similarly, changes in a company's working capital also impacts its cash flow. Working capital is the difference between a company's current assets (cash, accounts receivable and assets expected to be converted to cash) and its current liabilities (accounts payable and short-term debts). Positive working capital means a company is in a position to meet its obligations in the short-term. A change in working capital from the previous period to the current period means the company has either increased its current assets or decreased its current liabilities. This can be achieved by managing current assets efficiently or paying down current liabilities.

Therefore, cash flow calculations also incorporate changes in working capital.

Adding to net income both D&A and changes in working capital produces operating cash flow (OCF).

Net Income + D&A + Change in Working Capital = OCF

Free cash flow

To get to free cash flow we need to adjust for another cash expense, the company's capital expenditure (CAPEX). CAPEX represents investments in long-term assets (growth CAPEX) and expenditure related to maintaining long-term assets (maintenance CAPEX).

Capital expenditures are treated like asset purchases. When a company spends money on CAPEX, there is a reduction in the cash on its balance sheet. The cost of the CAPEX is then capitalised, meaning the cost is added to the company's balance sheet as an asset rather than being recognised as an expense on the income statement. Over time the capitalised asset is depreciated or amortised. Therefore, while operating expenses impact the income statement immediately, capital expenditure impacts cash flow immediately, but only impacts the income statement gradually through depreciation.

Let's consider an example. A company buys a machine. The cost is classed as growth CAPEX and is dealt with on the balance sheet. The company then pays for ongoing servicing and repairs of the machine. These costs are classed as maintenance CAPEX and are also dealt with on the balance sheet. Finally, the machine requires electricity to run. This cost is classed as an operating expense and dealt with on the income statement.

CAPEX is therefore directly linked to the balance sheet as it relates to the company's assets and their valuation, while operating expenses are not linked to the balance sheet and instead relate to the costs incurred to generate revenues.

As the net income calculation does not account for cash flow associated with investing in and maintaining assets, the calculation of FCF deducts CAPEX to reflect the impact CAPEX has on cash flow.

$$OCF - CAPEX = Free\ Cash\ Flow$$

The following Sankey diagram illustrates the calculation of FCF from net income. We will cover stock-based compensation shortly.

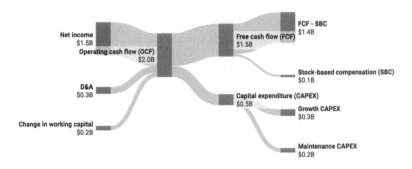

Capital light vs capital intensive businesses

All businesses sit on a spectrum between being capital light and capital intensive. The ratio of CAPEX-to-OCF gives a sense of how capital intensive a business is.

A low CAPEX-to-OCF ratio is seen in capital-light businesses. This indicates that the company is allocating a low amount of its cash flow to capital expenditure, often because the business requires minimal investment in tangible assets to generate revenue. This is normally because capital-light businesses rely more on intellectual property, technology and people, rather than heavy investments into physical infrastructure and manufacturing plants. Such businesses are often highly scalable, as they can expand their operations without having to make significant capital investments. Examples of capital-light businesses include software companies, online marketplaces and companies that outsource production to third-party manufacturers. Companies that are capital-light are often also asset-light, meaning that tangible assets, like property and equipment, represent a small percentage of their balance sheet.

A high CAPEX-to-OCF ratio indicates that the company is allocating a high amount of its cash flow to capital expenditure. This is often seen in manufacturing, oil and gas exploration and airlines. Growing such businesses is met with the resistance of requiring high capital expenditure. Companies that are capital intensive are often also asset-heavy, meaning that their tangible assets represent a high percentage of their balance sheet.

So to recap:

- **Capital light**: expenditure on physical assets is minimal.

- **Capital intensive**: expenditure on physical assets is significant.

- **Asset light**: physical assets are a minimal part of the balance sheet.

- **Asset heavy**: physical assets are a significant part of the balance sheet.

Companies actively expanding and investing to grow their business, may even have a higher CAPEX than OCF, which will result in a negative FCF. While negative FCF over the long-term is not desirable, over the short-term it can indicate expansion and investment for the future. Therefore, it is crucial to understand the reason behind negative FCF and additionally factor in the company's financial health, profitability and future growth prospects when drawing conclusions.

As operating cash flow includes capital expenditure, free cash flow is typically a more volatile figure. Despite this, FCF's strength lies in the fact that it represents the cash available to the company after accounting for investments in its assets.

When calculating a company's free cash flow it's important to consider one-off transactions, such as a one-off sale of an asset, a one-off investment in an asset or a one-off loss related to unusual events (e.g. natural disasters, legal settlements). While impacting FCF in the short-term, such one-offs are non-recurring revenues or costs, and will therefore not be seen in future years. Other non-recurring factors that may need to be taken into account are restructuring costs (e.g. layoffs and plant closures), M&A costs, non-recurring tax expenses or benefits, and changes in accounting policies. Accounting for these one-offs should help create a normalised view of a company's FCF.

Internal growth (organic) vs external growth (M&A)

A company has two options when it comes to investing in its growth. It can either invest internally or externally.

Organic growth refers to growth from investing internally. The purpose of internal investment is typically for either launching new and improved products or services (to help keep competition at bay) and for increasing business efficiency (to attain higher profits from lower costs). The return on such investment should be revenue growth, strengthening pricing power and increased operating efficiency. Famous examples of organic growth, include Apple's continuous investment in the development of innovative new products (e.g. the iPhone, iPad, iMac and Apple Watch), and Amazon's expansion from being an online bookstore to investing in logistics, distribution services, web services and streaming media.

In contrast, mergers and acquisitions (M&A) is growth through investing externally to either merge with or acquire other businesses. This can involve either acquiring competitors to enable growth in market share (horizontal integration) or acquiring suppliers and distributors to enable increased supply chain control (vertical integration).

A famous example of horizontal integration was Disney's 2006 acquisition of Pixar. Both companies competed in the animated film industry. The acquisition allowed Disney to increase its market share and to benefit from Pixar's technology, intellectual property and content.

An example of vertical integration is Apple's 2012 acquisition of AuthenTec, a company specialising in fingerprint sensor technology. AuthenTec had been a supplier to various companies, including Apple. By acquiring AuthenTec, Apple was able to integrate fingerprint recognition technology into their devices and importantly gain control over a critical component of their products. This acquisition helped Apple solidify their position as an innovator in smartphone security.

M&A doesn't have to be in the same industry or sector. The telecommunication company AT&T's acquisition of the media and entertainment company Time Warner brought together AT&T's distribution and communication services with Time Warner's vast portfolio of content, including HBO, CNN, and Warner Bros. This merger aimed to create a more integrated media and telecommunications company that could offer a combination of content and distribution services to consumers, giving AT&T control over both the creation and delivery of content.

Capital expenditure is associated with organic growth, as it represents investments the company is making in its operations. As FCF excludes capital expenditure, FCF already reflects a company's reinvestment in itself for organic growth. Companies are then free to use their FCF for a range of purposes, including M&A.

Free cash flow per share

As we have now seen, for multiple reasons it is harder for accountants to manipulate FCF than net income. This is because FCF is based on actual cash inflows and outflows, and therefore doesn't factor in depreciation and amortisation, but does factor in capital expenditure and changes in working capital.

In his book "Accounting for Growth", fund manager Terry Smith explains that "profits can be manufactured by creative accounting, but creating cash is impossible". He then summarises that "profits are someone's opinion, whereas cash is a fact."

During stock market bubbles, many investors (particularly investors in start-ups and IPOs) overlook free cash flow, and instead focus on estimates of a company's total addressable market and whether the company is growing its users and subscribers. When economic downturns happen, reality sets in again that ultimately it is FCF that matters.

As FCF is harder to manipulate, it is often seen as the most suitable metric for measuring growth. But there's still one last adjustment required to get to the best financial metric for assessing growth. This final adjustment is calculating the free cash flow per share. This involves dividing the free cash flow by the total number of shares outstanding that the company has.

Free Cash Flow / Shares Outstanding = Free Cash Flow per share

This represents the amount of free cash flow generated for each of the company's shares.

Stock-based compensation and share buybacks

The benefit of calculating FCF on a per share basis is that it allows us to account for any changes in the total number of shares issued by a company. A company's total number of shares can change as a result of new share issuances, stock-based compensation and buybacks.

Companies often issue new shares. An issuance of new shares will either bring in or not bring in fresh capital. When an issuance does raise money (e.g. an Initial Public Offering or a follow-on offering), new investors pay for the shares, which injects fresh capital into the company. While the total number of shares increases, each shareholder's ownership stake retains its proportional value because the capital raised has increased the company's resources.

When an issuance doesn't bring in fresh capital, then the newly issued shares have the effect of diluting a shareholder's interest in a company because the same amount of free cash flow is now shared between more shareholders. A shareholder's stake in the company therefore becomes smaller. This can lead to a decrease in free cash flow per share, since the FCF is now divided among a larger number of shares.

A lot of companies, especially early-stage ones, provide their employees with stock-based compensation (SBC). As a non-cash expense, SBC does not involve any actual cash outflow. Instead, it represents the cost of providing equity-based compensation. While great for incentivising staff and retaining talent, this has the effect of diluting a shareholder's equity and the FCF belonging to them. When a company issues SBC, it grants employees (and other stakeholders entitled to SBC) the right to acquire shares. When these stock options are exercised, new shares are issued, which increases the total number of shares outstanding. This impacts existing shareholders by diluting their ownership. SBC becomes especially relevant if the issuance of new shares is substantial compared to the value of its free cash flow. Companies typically disclose SBC in their financial statements, which can provide insights into these potentially dilutive effects on ownership.

To reverse the effects of shareholder dilution, companies often engage in stock buyback programmes (also known as share repurchases). This is when companies use cash to repurchase their own shares on the open market. This has the effect of reducing the number of outstanding shares, which can boost FCF per share. Buybacks can be an example of efficient capital allocation when shares are undervalued. However, they can also represent a misallocation of resources when the money could be used more efficiently by investing for the future.

There are two options for accounting for the effects of stock-based compensation and stock buybacks. Calculating FCF per share is useful when measuring growth, as it accounts for any share dilution caused by SBC and any reversal of share dilution by buybacks. As we will see in the chapter on valuation, subtracting SBC from FCF is useful when doing valuation as it better reflects the FCF belonging to shareholders.

Getting from revenue to FCF per share

So to summarise, the journey from revenue to FCF per share is as follows:

Revenue
- Cost of Revenue
- Operating Expenses
- Interest Expenses
- Tax
+ Depreciation & Amortisation
+ Change in Working Capital
- Capital Expenditure
/ Share Outstanding
= Free Cash Flow per share

The principle here is the calculation of FCF requires differentiating between cash expenses and non-cash expenses. Not all company expenses involve an outflow of cash. Cash expenses involve an actual outflow of cash, while non-cash expenses (also called accounting expenses) do not involve an outflow of cash.

Cash expenses include the cost of revenue, operating expenses and capital expenditure. These expenses all involve an outflow of cash and directly reduce a company's cash balance. Non-cash expenses include depreciation and amortisation and stock-based compensation. These expenses do not involve an outflow of cash.

Free cash flow is the final figure after subtracting cash expenses and ensuring that non-cash expenses are not subtracted.

As the name implies, free cash flow is cash that has flowed into the company and is now free for the company to use as it chooses, either to:

- Buy other companies (M&A)

- Buy back its own shares

- Pay down its debt

- Pay out a dividend to its shareholders

- Retain as cash on the balance sheet

The importance of FCF per share

FCF per share is recognised as a powerful metric by several business leaders and investors.

Rich Templeton, the CEO of the semiconductor company Texas Instruments, says that "the best measure to judge a company's performance over time is growth of free cash flow per share". It is his view that FCF per share growth is what "drives long-term value" for shareholders. Similarly, Jeff Bezos, the founder of Amazon, is also of the view that "it's the absolute dollar free cash flow per share that you want to maximise". Lastly, Dev Kantesaria of Valley Forge Capital Management says that he thinks of "free cash flow per share growth as the primary metric correlated with intrinsic value growth".

Academic studies have shown that companies that convert a high percentage of their earnings into FCF outperform the companies that convert a low percentage of earnings into FCF. One such paper, titled "Are Cash Flows Better Stock Return Predictors than Profits?", demonstrated that companies with high levels of cash flow outperform those with low levels of cash flow. The paper concludes that investors may be able to obtain better stock returns by relying on cash flows rather than measures of profitability from the income statement.

The sum total of the evidence demonstrates that, above all, every business, regardless of sector and the products and services sold, should be judged as being in the free cash flow generating business. If it doesn't have a cash flow, then it doesn't have a business.

Visa, the credit card company, is a great example of a company that has consistently grown its FCF per share over a long period of time. Over the last 15 years (2009-2024), Visa has grown its FCF per share at an average rate of 37% per year.

The following chart demonstrates just how consistent this growth has been. Applying an exponential regression to the data reveals a correlation of 0.95, which is fairly good for real world data.

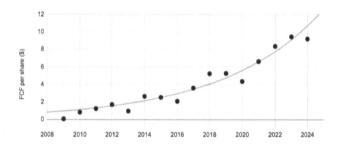

Where FCF growth has gone, share price has followed. Over the same time period share price grew annually by 23% per year. The fact that Visa's FCF per share growth (37%) has outpaced its share price growth (23%) over this time period is due to the company's FCF yield increasing over this time period.

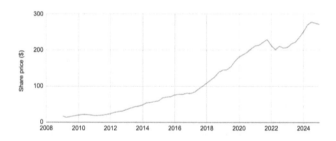

Long-term consistent FCF per share growth

For the purposes of evaluating a company, it is important to understand a company's FCF per share growth over a long time period, ideally 10+ years. Like we did earlier, we can employ linear and exponential regression analysis to FCF per share growth to help identify the companies that have consistently grown their FCF over long time periods with low levels of volatility. This approach removes companies where growth has been cyclical, meaning we can focus on long-term growth with low volatility. The following table sets out a list of companies that have enjoyed both high and linear FCF per share growth between 2009-2024.

Company	15yr FCF CAGR	Linearity
Visa	37%	0.95
Mastercard	29%	0.97
Apple	22%	0.96
REA Group	22%	0.98
Vitrolife	22%	0.96
Alimentation Couche-Tard	20%	0.96
UnitedHealth	16%	0.95
Hexagon	15%	0.98
Rollins	14%	0.95
Manhattan Associates	13%	0.95
Heico	13%	0.97
Intercontinental Exchange	13%	0.97
Verisk	11%	0.97
Waste Connections	11%	0.96
Factset Research	10%	0.97
Verisign	9%	0.96
ANSYS	9%	0.98
Church & Dwight	9%	0.96
Accenture	9%	0.95
IDEX Corp	9%	0.97
Paychex	7%	0.96

Correlation allows us to find the companies that have growth that is both high and predictable. The below quadrant divides companies based on their rate of growth and predictability of growth. Investors in quality growth companies typically focus on the companies in the top-right, where growth is high and predictable.

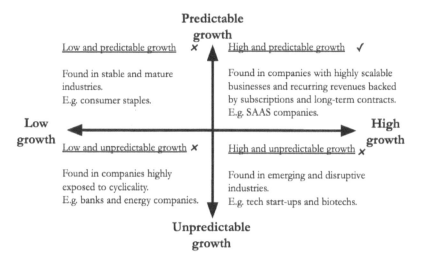

Determining a company's FCF per share growth is only the first step in our analysis. It's important to understand the trends that produced the growth in the past and to reach a view on whether growth can continue into the future. Ideally a company will have multiple drivers of future growth. For example, the semiconductor industry looks set to benefit from AI, cloud computing, data centres, smart phones and electric vehicles. The more growth drivers the better.

Chapter 3:
FCF margins
(Value creation)

Companies and their supply chains

Businesses have suppliers and customers. They:

- buy raw materials and pay for services from their suppliers,

- add value to what they take in through the creation of their products and services, and then

- sell the value-added products and services to their customers.

An effective relationship with the supply chain is reflected in a consistently high profit margin. A high profit margin requires both the ability to keep prices high and to keep costs low.

Margins measure a company's ability to generate value and control costs. There are two types:

- **Profit margins**: e.g. gross profit, operating profit, net income and free cash flow, calculated as a percentage of revenue.

- **Expense margins**: e.g. cost of revenue, SG&A, R&D and CAPEX, which reflect expenditure relative to revenue.

The following Sankey diagram demonstrates that profit margins decrease as you work down the income statement from revenue to net income.

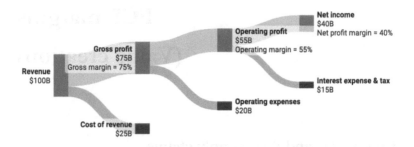

If a company generates $100bn in revenue and $75bn in gross profit (like in the above Sankey diagram), then the company has a gross margin of 75%. This means that the company makes things for $25, adds a $75 markup and sells them for $100. It's obviously better to be able to make something for $25 and sell it for $100 (a 75% gross margin), than it would be to make something for $80 and sell it for $100 (a 20% gross margin).

Margins reflect both pricing power with customers (i.e. the ability to raise prices) and bargaining power with suppliers (i.e. the ability to minimise costs). A high profit margin means the company is adding a high mark up to what they're selling. This suggests that if a company had to, it could drive future growth by lowering its prices, thus applying a lower markup and reducing its profit margin. Lowering prices isn't the ideal long-term strategy for fueling growth, that would be selling more while raising prices, but the ability to eat into already wide margins does suggest that the company has a future ahead of it.

It's worth noting that margins and growth can be understood at both the level of the entire organisation and also at the level of individual business areas, such as each product and geographic market. For example, a company's main product may generate higher margins and higher growth than its other products. Similarly, a company might see stronger growth in one geographic region due to favourable economic conditions or a more favourable competitive position, while in other regions they may lag behind. For example, Amazon dominates the internet retail market in the U.S. and many other regions, but its presence is less pronounced in parts of Asia, where local giants like Alibaba and Shopee lead the e-commerce landscape. Therefore, in certain instances to get the full picture it may be necessary to look beyond the headline profit margin and also assess the performance of a company's individual segments.

The following Sankey diagrams illustrate the income statements for Visa and Intel. You will notice that Visa retains a lot of its revenue as gross profit (gross margin = 74%) and a lot of its gross profit as operating profit (operating margin = 65%).

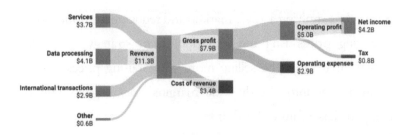

In contrast, Intel has comparatively a higher cost of revenue and therefore retains less revenue as gross profit (gross margin = 34%). Intel is also running an operating loss and therefore has neither any operating profit nor net income. These charts demonstrate that Visa has comparatively stronger margins than Intel.

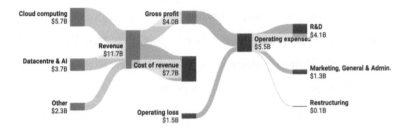

FCF margin

We've already established that free cash flow is the preferred metric for measuring growth. Free cash flow is also an effective numerator when calculating margins.

The FCF margin is a company's free cash flow divided by its revenue and expressed as a percentage. It is the measure of the amount of cash generated by a company as a proportion of its revenue.

$$FCF\ Margin = Free\ Cash\ Flow\ /\ Revenue$$

Ultimately the FCF margin indicates the amount of value a company is creating for its supply chain. It tells you how much cash the business is generating from its sales. If a company has a FCF margin of 40%, then for every $100 in sales it keeps $40 as cash.

High FCF margin sectors and companies

The following table is a list of companies that have managed to maintain a very high average FCF margin over a 10 year period.

Company	10yr avg. FCF Margin
Verisign	53%
ATOSS Software	51%
Bioventix	47%
Rightmove	46%
Eurofins Scientific	45%
Text	44%
Kinsale Capital Group	41%
Texas Pacific Land	41%
Mastercard	34%
Visa	33%
REA Group	32%
ANSYS	28%
Paychex	27%
Hong Kong Exchanges and Clearing	27%

Novo Nordisk	27%
Microchip Technology	27%
Descartes Systems	26%
Microsoft	25%
MSCI	25%
Adobe	24%
Keyence	23%
Factset Research	23%
Experian	23%
Apple	23%

Margin expansion and growth

It's important when studying a company's growth to consider its margins and whether they are expanding or shrinking. Ideally a company shouldn't just have profit margins that are high, but also profit margins that are expanding.

Mettler Toledo, the weighing equipment manufacturer, is a great example of a company that has consistently grown its margins. The following table sets out Mettler's growth profile over the last 10 years from top-line revenue growth all the way down to share price appreciation. You will notice that the compounded annualised growth rates (CAGR) increase as you move from left to right of the table.

	Revenue	Gross profit	Op. profit	Net income	FCF	FCF per share
CAGR	5%	6%	9%	10%	13%	16%

So how is it possible that 5% annualised revenue growth can become 16% annualised free cash flow per share growth? Multiple factors have come together to contribute to this impressive growth profile. Selling more, raising prices and cutting costs allowed Mettler Toledo to grow their net income faster than their revenue. Efficient management of working capital and low capital expenditure allowed them to grow free cash flow faster than net income. And share buybacks allowed them to grow FCF per share faster than FCF. The below graphic sets out how these factors come together to boost share price appreciation. These factors will be expanded upon in the chapters that follow.

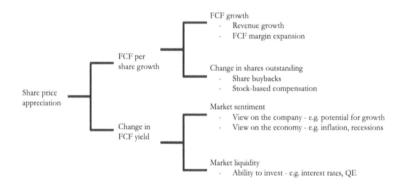

Operating leverage

Companies that can grow their revenue without significantly growing their costs benefit from operating leverage. This requires a company to have managed to arrange for a large proportion of their costs to be fixed, rather than variable. Therefore, as revenue increases, the company benefits from an even larger increase in free cash flow.

Operating leverage can mean that a 1 percentage point increase in revenue growth leads to a more than 1 percentage point increase in FCF, and conversely, a 1 percentage point decrease in revenue can lead to a larger percentage decrease in FCF.

Sectors with high operating leverage, such as technology and software, benefit more having a large proportion of their costs being fixed. Once they cover their fixed costs, any additional revenue is then profit, leading to higher margins as sales grow. It is extremely hard for other sectors, particularly banks and companies exposed to commodity prices, to benefit from operating leverage, as their costs are heavily influenced by interest rates and commodity markets, and therefore tend to be more variable. A 2021 paper titled "Operating leverage and stock returns under different aggregate funding conditions" found that companies with operating leverage typically outperform, especially in an low interest rate environment when there aren't any constraints on funding. The authors note that operating leverage can be a source of risk, particularly when moving out of a low interest rate environment where funding constraints return.

The types of cash and non-cash expenses incurred by companies

Profit margins, such as the gross margin, operating margin and FCF margin, are used to analyse long-term profitability trends. In contrast, expense margins, such as the R&D margin and CAPEX margin, are used to analyse long-term expenditure trends.

The R&D margin (R&D / Revenue) is important for tech and pharma companies as it indicates how much revenue needs to be invested in R&D to drive future growth. The CAPEX margin (CAPEX / Revenue) indicates how much revenue is reinvested into long-term assets, with a high margin suggesting that the company is capital-intensive and reliant on physical infrastructure. The SG&A margin indicates how much revenue goes to overheads, with a high margin suggesting possible inefficiencies that could be improved. A high marketing margin indicates a possible reliance on advertising to maintain brand strength and drive growth. A high interest expense margin suggests a reliance on debt to drive growth.

The following table sets out for each of the main expenses the sectors and industries that typically have the highest costs for each category.

Type of expense	Types of business where expense is high
Cost of revenue	Manufacturers of physical goods often have high costs associated with raw materials, labour and production. Retailers of physical goods typically have high costs associated with inventory and distribution.
Sales and marketing costs	Tech and consumer companies often invest heavily in sales and marketing to establish their brand and gain market share.
General and administrative costs	Healthcare and financial services companies typically have high administrative costs associated with regulatory compliance and reporting.
Research and development	Pharmaceutical, biotech and tech companies often have high R&D costs related to the development of new products in order to stay competitive.
Depreciation and amortisation	Manufacturers, energy and utilities companies typically rely on physical assets, which are often subject to ongoing depreciation.
Interest expenses	Capital intensive industries that involve high borrowing costs, such as energy and real estate companies, often have significant interest expenses.
Tax	The geopolitical nature of the oil and gas industry means that such companies can face complex tax regulations. Multinational companies also have higher tax expenses due to global operations and varying international tax laws.
Capital expenditure	Companies reliant on physical assets and infrastructure, such as telecommunications, energy and utility companies, require CAPEX to expand and maintain their operations.
Stock-based compensation	Start-ups and growth companies, often found in the tech sector, use stock options and equity compensation schemes to attract and retain talent.

Having considered how company's add value to their supply chain, we can now consider how they add value for their investors.

Chapter 4:
FCF return on capital
(Capital efficiency)

The capital lifecycle

Companies need capital to buy assets and to invest in projects. In the context of corporate finance, capital takes two forms: debt and equity. In the context of financial markets, these two forms of capital are known as bonds (debt) and shares (equity). When a company needs money, it will issue one or both of these types of capital, which are then bought by investors. Once the company has the money it needs, it can then engage with its supply chain.

The lifecycle of a company's capital is therefore as follows. A company will:

1. Borrow money from debt and equity investors,

2. Exchange the money with suppliers for goods and services,

3. Provide goods and services to customers in exchange for payment, then

4. Return surplus profits to their investors in the form of repayments and dividends.

The more profitable a company is, the more profit they will have to share with shareholders.

The following simplified diagram helps visualise this concept.

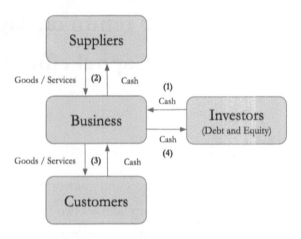

Businesses don't operate in a vacuum. There are other businesses out there competing for investors, suppliers and customers.

Businesses, therefore, have three key relationships:

1. **Relationship with investors**: i.e. the shareholders and lenders. An effective relationship with investors is reflected in a consistently high return on capital (covered in this chapter).

2. **Relationship with supply chain**: i.e. the suppliers and customers. An effective relationship with the supply chain is

reflected in a consistently high profit margin (covered in the previous chapter).

3. **Relationship with competition**: i.e. businesses that compete for the same suppliers and customers. A superior relationship over competitors is reflected in pricing power (covered in the next chapter).

The objective and three rules of corporate finance

Corporate finance is the area of finance that concerns:

1. **How a company should fund itself**: i.e. how it raises capital from investors.

2. **How it should invest its capital**: i.e. which assets it buys and which projects it invests in.

3. **How it should manage any capital it doesn't need**: i.e. its policy for returning excess profits to shareholders in the form of dividends and buybacks.

The objective of corporate finance is to maximise the value of the company. More narrowly, this can be understood as maximising the value of the company's shareholder equity, or even more narrowly, maximising the value of the company's share price. While some academics sometimes suggest that other objectives should also be considered, such as having a social purpose, ultimately it is maximising share price value that matters for a company's shareholders.

So what drives a company's share price? Growth in share price is driven by the company growing (e.g. FCF per share going up) and the company becoming more expensive (e.g. FCF yield coming down). Companies have little control over their market valuation (which will be covered in more detail in the chapter on valuation). Therefore, as established in the previous chapter, the number one objective in corporate finance should be maximising FCF per share.

This objective of maximising value is achieved by following the three rules of corporate finance:

1. **Invest in high return assets** - specifically income generating assets and appreciating assets.

2. **Use low cost debt** - to finance the purchase of the high return assets.

3. **Return capital to investors** - only if there are no suitable opportunities for reinvesting profits into high return assets.

The objective of maximising shareholder value relates more to the long-term than the short-term. In other words, a company shouldn't engage in activities that boost value in the short-term if they would be detrimental in the long-term.

The objective and three rules of corporate finance should be integral to how investors analyse companies and how investors manage their portfolios. The rules of corporate finance have two implications for investors. Firstly, when we analyse a company we should evaluate the extent to which the company's management follows the rules of corporate finance by considering (i) how high the return is on their assets, (ii) how low the cost is of their debt, and (iii) their framework for returning capital to investors. Secondly, like companies, our aim as investors when managing our investments should also be maximising total return (which takes into account both share price growth and dividends). This means we should not limit ourselves to investing in one country or one region of the world, one sector or industry, or one market capitalisation size. Instead, we should only focus on investing in assets with the greatest opportunity for the highest total return.

Return on capital

Three important concepts that are important to takeaway from this chapter are the definitions of capital allocation, capital efficiency and return on capital.

1. **Capital allocation** refers to a company's decision-making on where to invest its resources, i.e. the projects to invest in, the assets to buy and the companies to acquire.

2. **Capital efficiency** refers to how effective a company is at capital allocation to generate returns.

3. **Return on capital** is the measure, in percentage terms, of how capital efficient a company has been at capital allocation.

The best place for understanding how diligent a company is at corporate finance is to look at its return on capital (ROC). ROC is a measure of the return a company generates from its capital, thus revealing how efficient it is at using the capital it has raised from investors.

To create value a company's return on capital must be higher than its cost of capital. If a company can borrow capital at around 3% and can invest it at a return of 20%, then over time the company is creating value. If a company borrows capital at 3% but can only generate a return of 1%, then over time it is destroying value.

The MSCI World Quality Index tracks companies that have high returns on capital. From 1994-2024 this quality-focused index returned 11.87%, while the benchmark, the MSCI World Index, only returned 8.43%. Over the last 25 years, there has not been a single 10 year period when the quality index didn't outperform its benchmark.

This outperformance of quality appears to be seen in most regions. The below table compares the 10 year annualised return (2014-2024) of MSCI's index for each region alongside the corresponding quality index for that region. Interestingly, outperformance by the quality index was seen in all regions.

Region	Quality Index	Index	Difference
World	13.5%	10.1%	3.4%
USA	15.5%	13.1%	2.4%
Canada	3.9%	1.8%	2.1%
Europe	7.4%	5.4%	2.0%
Asia Pacific	6.7%	4.9%	1.8%
Emerging Markets	4.0%	3.0%	1.0%

China	1.5%	0.6%	0.9%
Australia	4.6%	4.2%	0.4%
Japan	10.9%	10.5%	0.3%
UK	3.5%	3.3%	0.2%

Balance sheets

Calculating the ROC involves comparing the income statement to the balance sheet. At this point it's worth pausing to consider what a balance sheet is. There are three main components: assets, liabilities and equity.

$$Assets = Liabilities + Equity$$

The following table is a stylised balance sheet of a typical company. Unlike income statements which reflect a period of time (typically 1 year), balance sheets are a moment in time snapshot of the financial condition of a business. A company's assets are set out on the left and its liabilities and equity on the right. The reason it is called a balance sheet is because assets always equals liabilities plus equity. If a company has more assets than liabilities, then its equity is positive. If a company has more liabilities than assets, then its equity is negative. In this way, equity ensures that the balance is maintained.

Assets	Liabilities	
Current assets	Current liabilities	
Cash and equivalents		Accounts payable
Short-term investments		Tax Payable
Accounts receivable		Short-term debt
Inventories		Deferred revenue
Non-current assets	Non-current liabilities	
Property, plant, equipment		Long-term debt
Goodwill		Capital leases
Other intangible assets		Deferred revenue
	Equity	
	Shareholder's equity	
		Paid-in capital
		Additional paid-in capital
		Retained earnings
		Treasury stock

Assets are what the company owns, and are made up of current and non-current assets. Non-current assets include tangible assets (e.g. machinery and buildings) and intangible assets (e.g. patents and brands), while current assets include cash, amounts owed by customers (receivables) and inventory.

$$Assets = Current\ Assets + Non\text{-}Current\ Assets$$

Liabilities are what the company owes. Its non-current liabilities are its long-term debt (e.g. bonds), while its current liabilities are its short-term debt.

$$Liabilities = Current\ Liabilities + Non\text{-}Current\ Liabilities$$

The term "current" refers to the timeframe within which assets are expected to be converted to cash or liabilities are expected to be settled. In this context it helps assess the short-term liquidity of a company, indicating its ability to meet short-term obligations with short-term assets.

Equity represents what would be left over if a company sold all its assets and paid off all its liabilities. Equity is the part of the company that belongs to shareholders. If a company were to sell its assets and pay off its liabilities, then the remaining cash (equity) is what would be returned to the shareholders. When you buy shares, it is the equity that you are purchasing.

$$Equity = Assets - Liabilities$$

Equity has four main components. Paid-in capital is the capital that shareholders put into the company when it was first incorporated. Additional paid-in capital represents the subsequent points in time where additional capital is paid in. Retained earnings represents profits or losses that have been retained by the company on the balance sheet, and not distributed as dividends. Lastly, treasury stock are the company's shares that were once tradeable in the open market, but have since been repurchased by the company, thus reducing the total outstanding shares in the market.

$$Equity = Paid\text{-}in\ capital + Additional\ paid\text{-}in\ capital + Retained\ earnings + Treasury\ stock$$

Invested capital represents the capital that shareholders and bondholders have both put into the company. It is the sum of the capital invested by shareholders (i.e. equity) and bondholders. (i.e.

non-current liabilities, which includes long-term debt, such as bonds). Together this is the capital used to finance the company.

$$Invested\ Capital = Non\text{-}Current\ Liabilities + Equity$$

Because of the nature of the balance sheet, it can also be calculated as follows.

$$Invested\ Capital = Assets \text{-} Current\ Liabilities$$

Real world balance sheets

The following Sankey diagram sets out the balance sheet of Visa. On the asset side, note the strong cash position and the fact that there are more intangible assets than property, plant and equipment. On the liabilities side, note the low long-term debt compared to equity. This illustrates that Visa is an asset-light, cash generative and well-financed business.

Visa

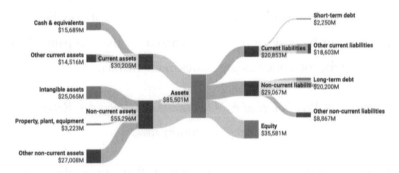

In contrast, the following Sankey diagram sets out the balance sheet of Bed, Bath & Beyond, shortly before it filed for bankruptcy in 2023. On the asset side, note the low levels of cash, lack of intangible assets and the considerable proportion of its assets as property, plant and equipment. On the liabilities side, note the high proportion of liabilities compared to the small slither of shareholder equity. This illustrates that a lot of debt was used to finance an asset-heavy business.

Bed, Bath & Beyond

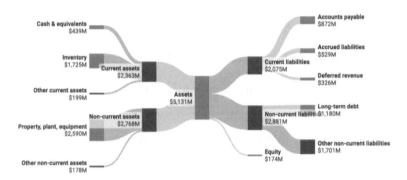

Calculating the return on capital

Comparing the income statement to the balance sheet reveals how efficient the company is at using its balance sheet to generate income (i.e. the return on capital).

There are several ways to calculate the return on capital. A common way is to calculate the return on equity capital. This means calculating net income as a percentage of equity. There are two shortcomings to this method. Firstly, in terms of the numerator of the equation (net income), we have already seen it is an accounting metric open to discretion in how it is calculated. Secondly, in terms of the denominator part of the equation, shareholder equity can also be distorted if large amounts of debt are used to boost a company's returns. The ideal metric should reflect the amount of cash returned for every dollar of capital invested into the business. Therefore, the preferred approach is to calculate the company's free cash flow return on its invested capital.

$$FCF\ ROC = Free\ Cash\ Flow\ /\ Invested\ Capital$$

Once expressed as a percentage, the number tells you how much cash the company generates for every $100 of capital invested.

Businesses that are capital-light and asset-light can keep capital expenditure low as they are not heavily reliant on capital to operate physical infrastructure and generate profit. Asset-light and capital-light businesses often outperform asset-heavy and capital-intensive businesses, given their ability to obtain higher returns on capital and maintain low capital expenditure.

Defying economic gravity

While a high return on capital is great, a consistently high value over a long period of time is even better. A lot can be inferred from a company that has been able to maintain a high return on capital for a long time.

The economic law of mean reversion suggests that a company with a high return on capital should see competitors infiltrate its market, offer a cheaper and/or better alternative and thus compete away the company's high returns. We can infer that the small number of companies that defy economic gravity and maintain a high return on capital over a long time period benefit from advantages over their competition.

When analysing a company, everything you learn about it is in the past, but its value lies in the future. While the future is always uncertain, companies with high returns on capital often see these high returns persist into the future. The asset management company, Schroders, showed in their paper "Why Quality Stocks Offer Higher Return and Lower Risk" that companies deemed as being high quality continue to enjoy high returns on capital and high profit margins for at least 2 years into the future. They conclude that the reason why quality companies are able to outperform is due to the quality of their fundamentals being persistent and not being easily eroded.

What we will see in the chapters that follow is that many quality companies enjoy pricing power, barriers to entry and other forms of resilience that allow them to be long-term creators of value. Such advantages aren't easily eroded.

The following table sets out the companies that have managed to average a free cash flow return on capital above 25% over the last 10 years.

Company	10yr average FCF ROC
Verisign	91%
Texas Pacific Land	69%
LVMH	65%
Manhattan Associates	64%
Fortnox	62%
Novo Nordisk	61%
TechnologyOne	42%
Ubiquiti	41%
Mastercard	40%
Intuit	38%
Paychex	36%
Apple	36%
Coloplast	35%
Pernod Ricard	33%
IDEXX	33%
Fortinet	32%
Autozone	32%
Kone	32%
Automatic Data Processing	31%
Home Depot	30%

A further complement to the above approach is to not only look for high returns on capital, but to also look for companies that never have low returns on capital. The following table lists companies sorted by how high their lowest FCF return on capital was over the last 10 years. These companies are therefore consistent compounders of their capital. For each one, it's safe to say they're doing something right.

Company	Lowest FCF ROC in last 10 years
Novo Nordisk	49%
Verisign	47%
Manhattan Associates	43%
Texas Pacific Land	35%
Mastercard	30%
Paychex	27%
TechnologyOne	24%
Accenture	23%
Autozone	23%
IDEXX	22%
Rollins	22%
Home Depot	21%
Automatic Data Processing	21%
Fortnox	21%
Apple	19%

Fortinet	18%
Experian	18%
Williams-Sonoma	17%
Mettler Toledo	17%
Expeditors International	17%

In the following chapter we will examine in more detail why such companies are able to maintain high returns on capital and high margins over the long-term.

Return on capital in different industries and sectors

As you will have noticed, there often aren't any airlines, banks or energy companies in the lists of companies that have high growth, high margins and high returns on capital. Instead such lists predominantly contain companies in the technology and healthcare sectors, and provide services to other businesses rather than directly to consumers. The following table sets out the annualised total return (share price return plus dividend income) from 1994-2024 for a range of industries and sectors.

Sector	Annualised Total Return (1994-2024)
Software	13.7%
Healthcare	10.8%
Household & personal items	9.7%
Energy	8.6%
Index	8.5%

Transport	7.0%
Banks	5.5%
Automobiles	5.1%
Communication services	4.4%

Sectors with low returns on capital are more than likely exposed to interest rates (e.g. banks), commodity prices (e.g. metal prices for miners, fuel prices for airlines, oil prices for energy companies), the economic cycle (e.g. the demand for business and recreational travel drops during a recession) and competitors (e.g. there are hundreds of banks compared to just two major credit card companies). In contrast, sectors that can maintain high returns on capital see consistent demand for their products (even during an economic slump), they are not overly exposed to interest rates or commodity prices, and exist in sectors where it's easier to create and maintain competitive advantages.

Morgan Stanley, in their paper "In Search of a Late-Cycle Buffer", provide a helpful illustration of how different sectors perform during recessions. They show that during the 2007-2008 Global Financial Crisis it was the healthcare, consumer staple and software companies that proved the most resilient, while banks, other financial institutions and consumer discretionary companies took the biggest hit to their earnings. Looking for resilient businesses, particularly those that have survived and thrived during recessions and even pandemics, is important when seeking companies that can maintain high returns on capital year in and year out.

Compounding capital

Growth and return on capital are intrinsically linked. The following table sets out what a return on capital of 20% looks like over a 5 year time period. In this example $100 is invested in year 0 and by year 5 there is a total return of $199 (ROI = 199%). After year 1, not only are returns being made on the original capital, there are also returns on the retained and reinvested capital.

Year	Capital	Return	ROC
0	$100	$20	20%
1	$120	$24	20%
2	$144	$29	20%
3	$173	$35	20%
4	$207	$41	20%
5	$249	$50	20%
	Total ROI: 199%	Return CAGR: 20%	Average ROC: 20%

This example demonstrates that, under ideal conditions, a 20% return on capital should equate to a 20% growth rate. A high ROC and a high growth rate should, theoretically, go hand-in-hand. In reality this is often not the case for a couple of reasons.

Part of the reason why is due to balance sheets, and therefore the invested capital number used as the denominator in the ROC equation, being dynamic and not static. The value of a company's invested capital is impacted by a range of factors, not just returns. On the asset side of the balance sheet, tangible assets are subject to depreciation, intangible assets are subject to amortisation and goodwill is subject to impairment. On the other side of the balance sheet, a company will typically issue more long-term debt and equity as they grow in order to finance future growth. These factors, in addition to the return on capital, can all impact the total value of invested capital in the ROC equation.

We will now consider three scenarios to be mindful of when evaluating returns on capital. The first arises when ROC is high, but growth is low. As we will see, this is the result of low reinvestment opportunities leading to high dividend payouts and low growth. The second arises when growth is high, but ROC is low. This is often seen in situations where increasing amounts of capital are required to generate growth. The third arises when a company's equity is negative. This situation requires additional analysis to determine whether the negative equity is indeed a concern.

Pitfall 1 - High ROC, Low Growth

High ROC and low growth is typically seen when a company lacks reinvestment opportunities.

In the previous table, the hypothetical company retains 100% of its profits, meaning that the $20 return made in year 1 is retained as capital and reinvested in year 2. In reality, most companies will return at least some of their profits to shareholders, either in the form of a dividend or share buybacks. A company's payout ratio is the percentage of its profits that it returns to shareholders. A high payout ratio means that the majority of the company's free cash flow is being paid out as a dividend.

$$\textit{Dividend payout ratio} = \textit{Dividend per share} \ / \ \textit{FCF per share}$$

Let's re-consider the hypothetical company that can generate a 20% return on capital, although this time let's see what happens when it has a 75% payout ratio (rather than 0% as before). Rather than the ROC and growth both equalling 20%, now growth is only 5%. By year 5 the original $100 investment has only generated a total return (share appreciation plus dividends) of $155. The ROI is therefore 155%, compared to 199% in the previous example when the payout was 0%. This lower return is because less earnings are being retained and reinvested, resulting in slower growth.

Year	Capital	Return	ROC	Payout Ratio	Payout
0	$100	$20	20%	75%	$15
1	$105	$21	20%	75%	$16
2	$110	$22	20%	75%	$17
3	$116	$23	20%	75%	$17
4	$122	$24	20%	75%	$18
5	$128	$26	20%	75%	$19
	Total ROI: 155%	Return CAGR: 5%	Average ROC: 20%		

The ideal investment is a capital-light compounder, meaning the company doesn't need to retain and reinvest profits in order to grow. It can therefore payout its excess cash (either as a dividend or as a buyback) without hindering its future growth. Consequently each year the return on capital goes up, as does its free cash flow and payouts. Such companies are exceptionally rare.

For the majority of companies, it's important to be mindful of the payout ratio as a high and increasing ratio suggests that the company lacks growth opportunities. It's also important to be mindful that a company can use payouts to keep its capital at a low level and therefore its return on capital at a high level. High payouts, either in the form of a dividend or share buybacks, have the effect of shrinking the size of a company's balance sheet. This is because it reduces the value of the company's assets as cash is paid out. The effect is that the return on capital is increased, not because of growth, but as a result of shrinking the company's balance sheet and therefore its capital. Such low growth companies are typically evidenced by both a high return on capital, a high payout ratio and a low FCF growth rate. For long-term compounding it's important that both high growth and a high ROC be in place.

The payout ratio therefore often reflects the maturity of the business. Many growth phase companies opt for a zero dividend policy and therefore have a 0% payout ratio, while many mature companies gradually increase their payout ratio as their reinvestment opportunities decline. This reflects the corporate finance principle that we considered earlier, in that when a company has reinvestment opportunities it should maximise them, and when a company lacks reinvestment opportunities it should return excess capital to investors.

How profit distribution fits into the capital lifecycle

Where a company is in its lifecycle can be understood in terms of its capital and whether they are:

- Raising capital,

- Reinvesting capital, or

- Returning capital.

Young companies raise capital, established companies reinvest capital and mature companies return capital. Quite often a company will sit in between two of these three stages and therefore will either be raising and reinvesting capital, or reinvesting and returning capital. The best investments are the companies that are either retaining earnings to reinvest at high returns, or companies that can grow with minimal reinvestment. Be cautious of companies that are both raising capital and returning capital, as this is typically not prudent capital allocation.

When considering whether to reinvest or return capital, a company needs to decide between investing in organic growth or M&A, or returning cash to investors through buybacks and dividends. The optimal order of capital allocation typically begins with reinvesting into organic growth, as this generates long-term value by expanding operations and improving a company's competitive advantages. If opportunities for organic growth are limited, then M&A can be considered for expansion and market consolidation. Buybacks would then follow, as they can be used to enhance shareholder value when shares are undervalued. Distributing excess cash as dividends should be considered last once other higher-return options have been exhausted. Prioritising in this order ensures capital efficiency and maximising shareholder returns.

Dividend reinvestment

One option for investors faced with a company that has a high return on capital, but also a high dividend payout ratio, is to reinvest the dividends by purchasing more shares in the company. This isn't ideal, as having the company reinvest for you saves on transaction fees and taxes. When a company reinvests on its investors behalf, investors benefit from the price-to-book (P/B) ratio. For example, if a company has a P/B ratio of 10, then that effectively means it costs $10 to buy just $1 of a company's capital. This is inefficient for investors looking to reinvest dividends, but very efficient for investors in companies that reinvest earnings, rather than paying them out. This is because every $1 of earnings retained as capital now has a market value of $10.

In summary, be mindful of companies that have high ROC, but low growth. This is typically due to a lack of reinvestment opportunities, therefore prompting the company to return a significant portion of its earnings to shareholders either as a dividend or through buybacks.

Predictable dividend growth

Even though dividends can reflect a lack of reinvestment opportunities, a long history of dividend growth suggests that the company has a prudent approach to capital management. This is particularly true when dividend growth is found alongside high FCF growth, high returns on capital and a moderate or low payout ratio.

S&P Global published a useful paper on this subject titled "A Case for Dividend Growth Strategies". The research revealed several useful findings. Firstly, the authors demonstrated that dividend growth stocks (i.e. companies with a multi-decade history of increasing their dividend) on average tend to be higher quality businesses. This is probably not a surprise given the financial strength and discipline required to make such an achievement. Secondly, while many companies decrease their dividend during recessions, dividend growth stocks are typically less volatile during recessions than the index. Again, this is probably not a surprise given how recession proof many quality companies are. The paper also makes an important distinction between dividend growth stocks and high yield stocks. High yields are often found in utilities, financials and real estate companies. These are sectors often associated with low growth and low metrics for quality. The market therefore values them as cheap, resulting in a high yield. In contrast, dividend growth stocks are typically found in healthcare, consumer, industrial and technology companies. These are sectors often associated with predictable growth, high metrics for quality and long-term durable competitive advantages.

The table below sets out a list of dividend growth stocks that have grown their dividends with high linearity (correlation > 0.95) over the last 10 years. The list is sorted by the compounded annual growth rate of the dividend. In addition to having a consistent dividend growth rate, these companies also score highly on other quality growth metrics, including having high returns on capital and low payout ratios (to ensure dividends are sustainable).

Company	10-yr Dividend CAGR	10-yr Linearity
Lam Research	46%	0.99
Broadcom	37%	0.98
Intercontinental Exchange	29%	0.99
Mastercard	27%	0.99
Danaher	27%	0.95
Watsco	24%	1.00
Zoetis	23%	0.95
Exponent	21%	0.99
UnitedHealth	21%	0.99
Lowes	20%	0.96
Pool Corp	19%	0.96
Amphenol	19%	0.97
Home Depot	18%	0.99
Visa	18%	0.98
Nasdaq	17%	0.99
Intuit	17%	0.99

Pitfall 2 - Low ROC, High Growth

It's possible for a company to have a low return on capital and still experience high growth, although this is rarely sustainable long-term. Low ROC and high growth is seen in companies that are forced to take on more and more debt in order to fuel growth. The effect is that the newly borrowed capital is put to work at decreasingly lower returns, and therefore even though there's growth, there are also declining returns on capital.

Let's model this using a hypothetical company.

This time we will lower the ROC to only 5%, while keeping the growth rate at 20%. In contrast to the previous two examples, where we started with $100 of capital, in this example we need to start with $400 to obtain the same numerical return of $20. As ROC is 5%, naturally the growth rate should be inclined to be 5%. However, to keep the growth rate high, the company needs to take on more and more capital. In the real world this would be through either issuing more debt, thus increasing the leverage on the balance sheet, or issuing more equity and therefore diluting shareholders. The impact of requiring more and more capital to fuel growth is that even though returns are going up, the return on capital remains low. In this example $846 was invested ($400 in initial capital plus $446 in new capital) and a total return of $199 was generated. This is a ROI of just 23%, compared to 199% for when ROC and growth both equal 20%, and a ROI of 155% for when ROC is 20% and growth is 5%.

Year	Capital	Return	ROC	New Capital
0	$400	$20	5%	
1	$480	$24	5%	$60
2	$576	$29	5%	$72
3	$691	$35	5%	$86
4	$829	$41	5%	$104
5	$995	$50	5%	$124
	Total ROI: 23%	Return CAGR: 20%	Average ROC: 5%	

The following table sets out the total return on investment over 5 years from the three examples we just considered. High returns are found when there is a high ROC, and the highest returns are found when there is both a high ROC and high growth present.

	ROC	Growth	Total ROI
High ROC + High Growth	20%	20%	<u>199%</u>
High ROC + Low Growth	20%	5%	<u>155%</u>
Low ROC + High Growth	5%	20%	<u>23%</u>

The below quadrant summarises the above examples. It demonstrates that it's essential that a high ROC and a high growth rate both be in place to compound capital at the highest rates of return.

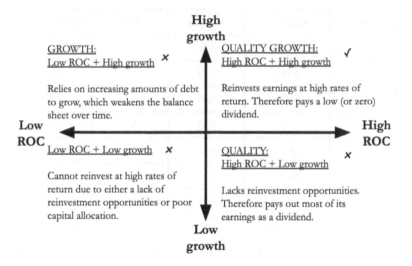

Pitfall 3 - Leverage and negative equity

While a high return on capital implies that a company is both profitable and uses its capital efficiently, it is important to consider the relationship between a company's equity capital and debt capital.

There are two ways to assess a company's debt: either using the balance sheet or using the income statement.

Starting with the balance sheet, companies can finance their assets with equity and/or debt. The ratio of assets-to-equity is known as leverage. The less debt, and therefore the more equity, a company has on its balance sheet, the less leveraged the company is. If a company has $80 of equity for every $100 of assets, then its leverage is 1.25x (100/80=1.25). If a company has $20 of equity for every $100 of assets, then its leverage is 5x (100/20=5). The latter company is therefore more highly leveraged as it has more debt than equity. While leverage can help multiply a company's returns, highly leveraged companies come with risk, particularly if interest rates were to start to rise.

Analysis of a company's debt can also be further understood by looking at the income statement. As a quick re-cap, a company pays the interest on its debt using its operating profits (see the below Sankey diagram for a graphic representation of the income statement).

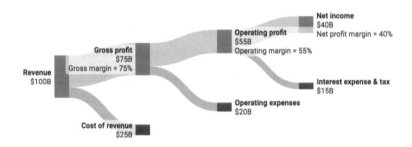

Evaluating a company's debt using the income statement involves dividing the interest expense (the amount a company pays in interest on its debt) by its operating profit (the amount the company earns before interest). This ratio is a measure of the affordability of the company's debt, with the lower the percentage the better.

Interest Expense Ratio = Interest Expense / Operating profit

While it's important that the percentage be low, it is also important to consider the long-term average. Calculating the 5-year average interest expense ratio allows you to assess whether the company's cost of borrowing has been stable, increasing or decreasing. A stable or declining interest expense ratio indicates a combination of effective debt management and favourable borrowing terms.

Occasionally you will come across a company that has negative equity. This is where the sum of a company's liabilities is greater than the sum of its assets. The reasons for negative equity can be wide ranging. If negative equity is the result of continuous financial losses, then bankruptcy may be inevitable. However, sometimes negative equity is the result of intangible assets being hard to value. If your view is that the intangible assets on a negative equity company's balance sheet have been undervalued in their accounts, then your own calculation of a company's assets may suggest that shareholder equity should actually be positive.

Negative equity can be the result of share buybacks, as repurchasing shares depletes a company's cash and therefore reduces its shareholder equity. The company could always sell back these shares to put the cash back on the balance sheet. When examining a company's balance sheet, under shareholder equity you may come across the item: treasury stock. When a company engages in share buybacks and repurchases its own shares, those shares are either retired (and no longer exist) or become treasury stock (and sit on the balance sheet). These repurchased shares are held by the company itself, which effectively reduces the number of shares outstanding to the public. Treasury stock represents a reduction in shareholder equity on the company's balance sheet. If buybacks are extensive, they can contribute to negative equity. But if they were to be sold again, then that would bring in cash and may return the company to positive equity. Buybacks can be particularly bad if a company overpays for its own shares or if it finances the buybacks by issuing more debt, thus increasing its liabilities.

Negative equity can also be the result of goodwill being impaired. The balance sheet item, goodwill, arises from mergers and acquisitions (M&A), particularly when a company pays more than the fair value. It appears as an intangible asset on the balance sheet and acts as a plug variable, to help balance the difference between the purchase price of the company acquired and the actual net value of the acquired company's assets. If a company overpays for an acquisition, then goodwill will inflate the total assets on the balance sheet. This artificially increases the amount of equity on the balance sheet, consequently reducing the return on capital. Goodwill is not amortised like other intangible assets. Instead it is subject to an annual impairment test. If it transpires that a company has overpaid, then goodwill may have an impairment loss recorded against it, which reduces its size on the balance sheet, and consequently can reduce a company's equity position. So be aware that if a lot of debt was used to finance an M&A transaction, then goodwill can temporarily support a positive equity position until the impairment loss is recognised, which could then push the company into negative equity.

So depending on the context, negative equity (and high leverage) may or may not be an issue. It is not an issue for companies that are able to meet their debt obligations as and when they arise, and therefore a low interest expense ratio suggests they're unlikely to default. Negative equity and high leverage become an issue when the company has a high interest expense ratio and is no longer able to meet its debt obligations.

Moving from financials to business models

Strong financial metrics, like a high growth rate and high margins and returns on capital, allow us to infer that a company is operating a quality business. But it is important that we support what we infer with a deep understanding of the company's business model. Once you understand why a company has strong financial metrics, you can then properly assess how likely those financial metrics will continue into the future.

We've so far considered two key relationships a company has: the relationship with its supply chain and the relationship with its investors. But there's still one more key relationship to consider, a company's relationship with its competitors.

Chapter 5:
Pricing Power

How to create pricing power and be a price setter, not a price taker

All goods and services are subject to the "elasticity of demand", meaning that at some point as price goes up, demand goes down. However, when price goes up, not all products see demand go down at the same point and at the same rate. This is because some products are inelastic, meaning demand changes minimally in response to price increases.

When a company consistently raises prices, eventually its customers will consider whether there are competitors providing a cheaper alternative. Companies with pricing power have the ability to consistently raise their prices, typically above the rate of inflation, without losing sales. This means their customers either don't or can't look for an alternative.

Customers put up with such price hikes for the following reasons:

- **The product has high utility and/or is highly desired**. Customers are more likely to tolerate price increases when a product has high utility or is highly desired. Products that are discretionary or offer low utility will likely face greater resistance to consistent price hikes. In contrast, products that are essential and <u>mission-critical</u> to a customer's operations are likely to face very little resistance to price hikes. High demand for a product is the foundation of pricing power. It enables companies to raise prices without losing customers. In some cases, price increases may even be a necessity in order to help manage demand.

- **No alternative exists (unique or rare product)**. When a company operates in a monopoly or duopoly, customers have little choice but to accept price rises due to the absence of competitors providing alternatives to choose from. The company is therefore in the enviable position of being a price setter, not a price taker. Occasionally the lack of an alternative may be because the company is the first entrant to a new market. In this instance the advantage may be short-lived. But more often, the lack of an alternative product is the result of the main provider being in a monopoly or a duopoly. If you want to book a flight or fill your car with fuel, then you have plenty of options to pick from. If you want a credit card or an operating system, then you will probably end up deciding between Visa or MasterCard, and Microsoft or Apple. Monopolies and duopolies often benefit from having <u>barriers to entry</u> that prevent new entrants to the market, and <u>barriers to scale</u> that limit the growth of any new entrants and inhibit their ability to scale up their business.

- **No better alternative exists (superior product)**. In some instances an alternative product is available, it's just of inferior quality. Companies can differentiate themselves from their competition by offering a better product. The ability to produce better quality products is called a <u>quality advantage</u> and requires continuous innovation, the development of unique features and strong brand reputation. When companies with a quality advantage raise prices, their customers are forced to stay as there are no alternatives of that same quality for customers to choose from. This is particularly effective in markets where customers are willing to pay more if they feel the higher price is justified due to the product's higher utility or desirability.

- **No cheaper alternative exists (affordable product)**. In some instances a good quality alternative is available, it's just more expensive. Companies can differentiate themselves from competition by offering a cheaper product. The ability to compete on cost is called a <u>cost advantage</u> and requires supply chain control, efficient production processes and economies of scale. When companies with a cost advantage raise prices, assuming they are still the cheapest option, there's no incentive for their customers to look for an alternative as there's not a cheaper alternative. If the product is already inexpensive (particularly in relation to the customer's other costs), then the customer will be less incentivised to find a cheaper replacement, even when there are price rises.

- **Switching is inconvenient (entrenched product)**. In some instances a cheaper and superior product may exist, but it's just inconvenient to switch providers. Companies with embedded products benefit from switching costs, which refers to the time, effort and risk involved in replacing the product. This switching cost could include logistical challenges, compatibility issues or the need to retrain staff. When changing providers isn't quick, easy and risk-free, customers will be hesitant to look for an alternative, given the time, cost, effort and risk involved. Therefore, price rises are put up with. Some companies create switching costs by becoming an essential part of their customer's supply chain. They customise their products to their customer's needs and provide a range of essential goods and services so that their customer's become fully dependent on them.

Utility, scarcity, quality, price and convenience all contribute to a company's ability to be a price setter. Once a customer is in a position that there isn't an alternative product, the supplier should then be in a position to introduce regular price hikes with little to no loss in sales.

How to succeed at value creation

Pricing power is integral to the value creation process.

As we saw in the earlier chapters, there are only three ways by which a company can increase its profitability (as per the income statement) and therefore create value. They are: (i) minimise the cost of raw materials, (ii) minimise operating costs and (iii) maximise revenue, either through selling more or raising prices.

Value creation, therefore, requires the ability to buy goods and services at a low cost, efficiently add value to what's taken in through the creation of the product and sell their finished product at a high markup.

Companies that consistently succeed at value creation and pricing power typically benefit from barriers to entry, barriers to scale, and other competitive advantages that allow them to succeed over the long-term.

We will now consider the three steps in value creation and what allows companies to excel at each step.

Minimising the cost of raw materials (supply chain control)

Companies that are able to succeed by competing on the cost of raw materials typically have one or more of the following traits:

- **The company benefits from having little reliance on raw materials**. Not all companies require large volumes of raw materials. This includes software companies, banks and insurers, professional services (e.g. lawyers and consultants) and marketing firms. Such businesses typically rely more on the creative expertise of their workforce and intangible assets. In contrast, asset-heavy and capital intensive businesses are more exposed to raw materials. For example, the automotive industry relies on large volumes of metals, construction companies require large volumes of cement and other building materials, and energy companies need large volumes of crude oil and natural gas. They rely on a steady supply of raw materials and their profitability is often tied to cyclical commodity prices, making it harder for them to consistently succeed at value creation.

- **The company benefits from having exclusive access to high-quality and/or low-cost raw materials.** Companies that are reliant on raw materials can thrive through having exclusive access to raw materials, particularly those that are either cheaper or of higher quality than those available elsewhere. Companies that benefit from such exclusivity are able to produce higher quality and/or cheaper products than their competition. Hermès, the luxury fashion brand, is able to source leather from some of the best tanneries in the world, through exclusive agreements. This is the result of vertical integration, meaning they own and have significant stakes in many of these tanneries. Vertical integration increases a company's control over their supply chain and reduces dependency on external suppliers. This integration can therefore create barriers for competitors, as potential competitors would require substantial investment and expertise to replicate the vertically integrated operations.

- **The company benefits from strong supplier relations**. By building strong, long-term partnerships with their suppliers, some companies are able to negotiate better prices and ensure a steady supply of high-quality materials. This can be through a combination of building trust and reliability, or even buying or investing in their suppliers. This not only reduces costs but also improves the stability of the supply chain. For example, ASML, the creator of advanced and critical equipment for semiconductor manufacturing, purchased a large stake in the optics company ZEISS to help ensure they continue supplying the high-performance optics that ASML relies on.

- **The company benefits from strong customer relations**. Ideally, a company's customers should want their supplier to succeed and thrive. This is markedly seen for monopolies and duopolies, as in the event the company were to go out of business, their customers would suffer significantly due to the lack of an alternative. Some monopolies and monopolies have even seen their customers, who otherwise would be in competition, instead work together to ensure that their supplier thrives and continues to provide the goods and services they need for their own survival. In particular, this has been seen with the semiconductor manufacturers that use ASML and the banks that use Visa. Interestingly, many of ASML's customers are also ASML shareholders, further supporting their strong market position.

- **The company benefits from economies of scale**. As a company increases how much it purchases from its suppliers, it is often able to negotiate better terms with its suppliers. As companies produce more they typically see their production costs go down on a per unit basis, as a result of fixed costs being spread across a larger number of units.

- **The company benefits from bargaining power**. Some suppliers only have one client or one main client. In this situation the client has bargaining power as the supplier is heavily reliant on its client for revenue. This helps when negotiating terms. The more customers a company has, the less reliant the company is on any one client for revenue.

Minimising operating costs (operational efficiency)

Once a company is in possession of their required raw materials, they must then get to work in turning those materials into the value-added products that their customers desire. Operational efficiency is the relationship between a company's input and output. Operationally efficient companies keep necessary costs low and avoid unnecessary costs.

Companies that are able to succeed by competing on operational costs typically have one or more of the following traits:

- **The company benefits from exclusive machinery and technology**. The creation of some products requires advanced machinery and technology. Automation can reduce labour and operational costs, allowing the company to compete on cost. If the machinery or technology is proprietary and protected by intellectual property, then this allows the company to create products that competitors aren't able to. If the machinery or technology is particularly expensive, and therefore requires a large upfront investment, then this capital requirement represents a further barrier to entry for competitors.

- **The company benefits from the expertise of their employees**. Companies often rely on the expertise of engineers and craftspersons. Technology and healthcare companies in particular require skilled professionals that are highly educated and qualified. Some companies are reliant on employees to be trained and knowledgeable at operating certain machinery or software. Companies also benefit from employees that are visionaries and innovative. Jony Ive, Apple's Chief Design Officer, played a pivotal role in the design of the iMac, iPod, iPhone, and iPad, which helped revive Apple's brand. In order to retain their top talent, companies need to provide training, incentivise innovation and reward their employees financially. Companies that aren't significantly reliant on raw materials, particularly software companies, are often more reliant on the talent and innovation of their employees.

Maximising revenue (market expansion and pricing power)

Having purchased raw materials and created the finished product, the company must now sell their product to their customers.

To maximise revenue the company must:

- maximise the number of units sold, and

- maximise the price that each unit is sold for.

Maximising units sold

Maximising the number of units sold requires the company to:

- increase its market share in existing markets, and

- enter new markets.

Increasing market share requires innovation and product differentiation in order for the company to set itself apart from competitors. Entering new markets requires strategy and planning. Entering new markets can involve geographical expansion, for example when Amazon expanded its operations from just the US to the rest of the world, and offered new products and services, such as Amazon Web Services (AWS) and Amazon Prime.

Maximising price

Maximising price requires pricing power, otherwise customers won't accept the higher prices and will look elsewhere.

When pricing power comes from a company being the sole provider or one of just two providers of a product (i.e. a monopoly or duopoly), we can infer that barriers to entry or barriers to scale are preventing additional competitors from entering the market and competing on market shares. When there are viable alternatives to a product, but customers still put up with price hikes, we can infer that there must be some form of switching cost, meaning there is a cost, effort or inconvenience stopping a company from changing suppliers.

Companies that are able to succeed by maximising revenue through flexing pricing power typically have one or more of the following traits:

- **Knowledge barrier: The company sells a product that competitors don't have the knowledge to recreate.** Companies can benefit from multiple layers of protection in the form of knowledge barriers. The recipe for Coca Cola remains one of the best kept secrets in the business world. It is protected by well-guarded trade secrets, only a select few employees know the complete formula, employees who are privy to the formula sign non-disclosure agreements (NDAs) so they are legally bound, the written formula is stored in a secure vault and different components of the formula are sourced from various suppliers preventing a single supplier deducing the entire recipe. This barrier means that competitors lack the knowledge to recreate the product.

- **Capability barrier: The company sells a product that competitors don't have the capability to recreate.** Certain products, particularly those that are technologically advanced, often benefit from their competitors not just not knowing how to recreate their product, but also lacking the capability to recreate their product. This can be the result of lacking the access to the required raw materials to make the product or lacking the infrastructure, technology or skilled workforce required to create the product. Even if you knew the recipe for Coca Cola, the infrastructure required to bottle and distribute the finished product at mass scale across the globe represents a near-insurmountable barrier to scale for most would-be competitors. Similarly, if you had a blueprint to make the latest iPhone, you would still face significant challenges in sourcing the components and assembling the device with the required level of precision. Overcoming the capability barrier requires a lot of upfront investment (resource barrier) or requires a lot of time and effort to create something that is hard to reproduce (time and effort barrier). We will consider these two types of barriers next.

- **Resource barrier: The company sells a product that competitors don't have the resources to recreate.** If you know how to create something and think you can develop the capability, then the next hurdle is finding the resources to develop the capability. A company that sells a product requiring significant resources to produce can deter would-be competitors due to the high costs and complexities involved. A great example of this is the Taiwan Semiconductor Manufacturing Company (TSMC). TSMC has invested tens of billions into having state of the art factories for producing semiconductors. TSMC has even benefited from state-level support from the Taiwanese government, in the form of subsidies, tax incentives and investment. The significantly high upfront cost of creating such factories impedes the ability of competitors to replicate what TSMC has achieved.

- **Time and effort barrier: The company sells a product that competitors are unwilling to put in the time and effort to reproduce**. Significant time and effort is often required to design and build both a product and a reputable brand, also to develop the capability to manufacture it. This is particularly true when it requires establishing a robust and complex supply chain that potentially spans countries and continents. The more time and effort required, the stronger the barrier to new entrants.

- **Network effect barrier: The company sells a product that increases in value as more participants use it**. A great example of the time and effort barrier is the network effect. Networks connect users, often buyers and sellers, and therefore can facilitate transactions. They are notoriously hard to create, but consequently are also hard to destroy. Networks can be monetised by the provider of the network taking a fee for making the transaction happen, e.g. the fees seen for using Visa and Mastercard's payment systems, fees for transacting on a stock exchange or fees for listing a product on an online marketplace. The value of the network increases as the number of users increases. More buyers attracts more sellers and vice versa. Creating a network requires not only creating the infrastructure, but also incentivising both buyers and sellers to join the network. There's a spectrum of network effects, meaning they range from being weak and vulnerable to being strong and fortress-like. Here are some factors to consider when evaluating the strength of a company's network. Strong networks often have:

— A growing number of new users,

— A high retention rate of existing users,

— A high and growing frequency of interactions between active users,

— A network effect where more sellers attract more buyers and more buyers attract more sellers,

— A reduction in costs per users as the network grows,

— A critical mass threshold, meaning a significant number of users is required in the first place for the network to be viable,

— A high user dependency, meaning users would find it costly or difficult to find an alternative,

— A diverse range of user types and transaction types (e.g. a stock market with a range of institutional and individual investors, a range of assets to buy, such as bonds, equities and commodities, and a range of transaction types to engage in, such as buying, shorting and borrowing), and

- Regulatory requirements, allowing the incumbent to stay as the dominant network.

- **Legal and regulatory barrier: The company sells a product that their competitors aren't allowed to sell.** Even if a company has the knowledge and capability to create and sell a product that could compete with one of their competitors, there are often other factors also in play. Intellectual property, such as patents and copyrights, can create legal protections that stop competitors from recreating the protected product. Holders of intellectual property can legally challenge infringers, deterring imitation. Patents provide temporary monopolies, which can help companies recover the costs they incurred when researching and developing their innovative products. Intellectual property portfolios can also generate revenue through licensing, making it expensive for competitors to use the protected assets. Heavily regulated industries, like banking and healthcare, can create formidable barriers to entry. This requires companies to have expertise to ensure compliance with relevant laws and rules, which inevitably comes with significant costs in the form of legal teams and technology to monitor and report compliance. Requirements to obtain regulatory approvals before certain products and services can be offered can create delays to market entry. Heavily regulated sectors can see innovation stifled and a hesitation from smaller innovators to enter the market.

In the event that a product has a better or cheaper alternative, customers will be less inclined to switch if the process of switching requires significant time and effort, is costly or risky. Companies that are able to succeed by maximising revenue through switching costs typically have one or more of the following traits:

- **Contractual barrier: The company sells a product to buyers that require long-term contracts.** Contracts are heavily negotiated legal documents that can represent significant revenue for a company and simultaneously be difficult to exit from, thus creating a barrier to entry for newcomers. A company might establish exclusive agreements with suppliers, ensuring that they are the only source for certain materials and components. Long-term contracts with customers can create stability and recurring revenue streams. New entrants would need to convince established customers to switch, which could prove to be challenging or impossible. Contracts can be hard for new entrants to replicate, giving established companies an advantage. While contracts can create barriers to entry, it's also worth noting that they can become subject to legal disputes, particularly if they are deemed as incompatible with competition law. Long-term contracts create a switching cost as there is typically a legal risk and cost attached to exiting a contract early.

- **Disruption barrier: The company sells a product that buyers would find disruptive to replace, e.g. customised components.** Many companies are heavily reliant on the goods and services they receive from their suppliers. Companies reliant on being supplied highly technical equipment typically require their workforce to be trained on how to use the equipment. Switching to alternative equipment would require their workforce to retrain, which costs the company time and resource. Switching can also entail compatibility issues. This occurs when a new system is not compatible with the existing system. For example, files created by existing software may not be openable by the potential alternative. These additional costs and adjustments can make switching less attractive, which benefits the company with the existing relationship. Companies often work closely together in the design of new products. Apple worked closely with the chip company Arm Holdings in the design of bespoke semiconductors for their iPhones. These are critical components for Apple that they can't obtain anywhere else, creating a competitive advantage for Arm Holdings over other chip companies. Collaboration not only facilitates continuous product improvement, it also optimises the supply chain and can help align production with demand. Integrated supply chains create a switching cost as switching to an alternative supplier would likely mean losing access to customised components, and would require having to reinvest time and energy into building a new supplier relationship.

- **Installed base barrier: The company sells a product to buyers that requires on-going servicing and maintenance.** Installed base refers to a company's product that is installed on its customer's property. This can refer to specialist equipment, such as scientific instruments, manufacturing equipment, elevators and even software. Companies with an installed base can generate consistent revenue streams through a servicing contract. For example, Rolls Royce engines in aeroplanes are serviced by Rolls Royce engineers and Kone elevators in tall buildings are serviced by Kone engineers. Companies with an installed base often have access to the specialist parts required for maintenance and are often positioned to benefit from their ability to gather valuable data and information from their clients, which should lead to improvements in the products and services they sell. Installed base creates a switching cost as it makes it costly (or even impossible) for companies to replicate the services and customer relationships that their competitors provide.

- **Brand barrier: The company sells a product in a market where buyers favour certain brands.** A strong brand provides consumers with familiarity, trust and risk mitigation. Brands allow consumers to outsource their decision-making, so that when they are selecting a purchase, rather than taking a risk by purchasing an item from an unknown brand, they can infer that a recognised brand means a higher quality product. This lowers search costs, as consumers don't have to risk the loss of time and money through searching for an alternative. Building a brand with a strong reputation takes time, investment and most importantly, consistent quality. Brands are particularly powerful when they confer legitimacy. A good credit rating from a well known agency like S&P and Moody's confers legitimacy on the issuer, which a start-up agency would lack. This legitimacy is important when issuing bonds as it lowers borrowing costs, meaning the issuer benefits by paying more for a well known brand. Brands can also create loyalty. Fans of Nike and Coca-Cola may be less likely to buy Adidas and Pepsi. Brand loyalty is the added value a brand brings beyond its functions and features. This means that a new entrant may find it challenging to compete solely on price or new and improved features. The loyalty that brands create mean that customers are less likely to switch to an alternative.

Barriers to entry and scale give companies the pricing power to maximise their revenues. But companies with pricing power should be careful not to exploit their position. Overpricing can incentivise customers to seek alternatives or develop their own alternatives, which can lead to a gradual erosion of a company's dominant market position. Overpricing can also trigger regulatory enforcement under competition law, particularly if a company is seen to be exploiting its dominant position. Instead, a company should take a strategic and long-term view to their pricing so that they are still efficiently creating value for shareholders, while not incentivising the erosion of their competitive advantages.

Bringing it all together

To recap the chapter so far, in order to grow profits a company must sell more, raise prices and cut costs. Selling more requires expanding operations in existing markets and entering new markets. Raising prices requires pricing power. Customers only put up with price rises if the product is essential and has high utility, doesn't have an alternative or the alternatives are lower quality, more expensive or inconvenient to switch to. Products that don't have an attractive alternative are typically produced by companies with barriers to entry and scale, meaning that competitors are unable to replicate the product because they don't know how to, don't have the capability to, don't have the resources to or aren't allowed to by law.

The below graphic sets out how pricing power, barriers and switching costs all come together to enable value creation.

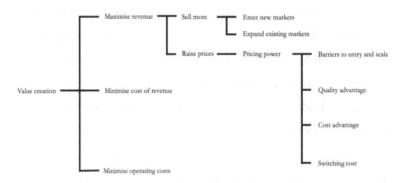

Value creation from the perspective of the income statement and balance sheet

Having considered how value creation is fueled by pricing power and barriers to entry, it is worth considering how value creation looks from the perspective of the income statement and balance sheet.

Value creation starts with companies borrowing money from investors (including both debt and equity investors). The company then purchases raw materials from suppliers, adds values to the raw materials in the creation of their product, and then sells their product to their customers. Ideally the profitability from this endeavour should be above the cost of the raw materials and other operating expenses. The profits generated should also represent a good return on the investment of the investors. The value creation process impacts the income statement and balance sheet differently. Pricing power allows companies to become highly profitable, both in relation to revenue on the income statement (creating a high margin), and in relation to invested capital on the balance sheet (creating a high return on capital).

In terms of the income statement, the cost of revenue (also known as cost of goods sold) captures the purchase of raw materials, operating expenses captures any expenses incurred during the value creation purchase (such as labour and overheads), and revenue captures the sale of the product. The higher the markup applied, the wider the profit margins and the more earnings and cash flow the company generates. Profit margins are therefore a good indicator of value creation.

In terms of the balance sheet, newly received capital will be cash on the asset side of the balance sheet and either a liability or equity on the other side of the balance sheet, depending on how it was financed.

- The purchase of raw materials sees cash go down and raw materials (classified as inventory) go up by the amount spent on the raw materials.

- The value creation process then sees raw materials go down, and finished products (also classified as inventory) go up by the cost of the raw materials and any additional operating costs incurred, like labour and overheads.

- The sale of the product then sees inventory go down and cash go up.

Assuming that the cash spent on creating the product is less than the cash generated in the sale of the product, equity (in the form of retained earnings) should also increase. The higher the markup applied, the higher the cash generated in proportion to the balance sheet and the capital borrowed from investors. Therefore, like profit margins, returns on capital are also linked to value creation.

Business resilience

Pricing power, barriers to entry and switching costs allow businesses to be resilient to competition. But competition isn't the only threat to a company's long-term profitability. In addition to resilience to competition, the ideal long-term investment should demonstrate resilience to industrial change, inflation, interest rates and economic cycles.

Business resilience: industrial change

There are plenty of companies that were resilient to competition, but were not resilient to industry change. Blockbuster was the dominant player in video rental and successfully fended off competition from smaller rental stores. However, their reliance on physical stores and failure to adapt to the shift towards streaming led to Blockbuster's collapse and allowed streaming providers to thrive. Similarly, Kodak was once an industry leader for cameras and film. Failure to embrace the rise of digital photography in time. Resilience to industry change is best supported by evidence of investment in R&D, and an ability and willingness of management to adapt to changing industries and embrace new technology.

Business resilience: inflation and interest rates

Inflation causes the price of goods and services to go up over time. Many central banks target a 2% inflation rate. Inflation is typically understood using the "basket of goods" concept. This is simply a hypothetical basket of commonly purchased consumer items. Assuming that central banks are successful in maintaining their 2% target, which is not always the outcome, then a $100 basket of consumer goods in 30 years time would be worth $181 ($181 = $100 x 1.02 ^ 30). In year 0, $100 cash gets you 100% of the basket of goods ($100 / $100). After 30 years of inflation, $100 cash only gets you 55% of the basket ($100 / $181). Therefore, the compounding of inflation has eroded away the purchasing power of $100, as over 30 years the purchasing power of $100 has dropped from one basket to 0.55 baskets.

If instead $100 was put into an equity fund, then using the historic annualised average growth rate of 8%, after 30 years the $100 investment would be worth $1,006 ($1,006 = $100 x 1.08 ^ 30). After 30 years, this is equivalent to 5.5 baskets of goods ($1,006 / $181). Unlike the first example, in this second example, investing has compounded purchasing power and not eroded it. Ultimately, the aim of investment is to compound your purchasing power and therefore hedge against the risk of it being eroded away by inflation.

The best protection against inflation is to own companies that have pricing power and can raise prices above the rate of inflation. As long-term investors we want companies that are price setters, not price takers. Oil companies are ultimately price takers, as they can't control the price of oil, which is set externally by the global oil market. Likewise, commercial banks are price takers as they can't control the interest rate set by central banks.

Companies with pricing power are price setters. They are typically insulated from commodity prices and interest rates, and can consistently raise their prices over time, often above the rate of inflation, without seeing a decrease in demand for their product. When inflation climbs, companies with pricing power are able to pass any increased costs resulting from inflation on to their customers. A consistently high margin signals that a company can insulate itself from inflationary shocks to the supply chain, such as a rise in oil prices, as it can eat into its margin by cutting costs, all while staying profitable.

Central banks respond to high inflation by raising the interest rate. Given that central banks can't control the supply side of the economy, the theory is that raising interest rates and making the cost of borrowing more expensive should place downward pressure on the demand side of the economy. The best protection against an interest rate shock is to own companies that aren't reliant on borrowing to finance their growth. This is particularly important if external finance were to become expensive due to interest rates and bond yields rising. If a company has a high return on capital, then it is able to reinvest its earnings and self-finance its growth. The company is therefore less reliant on external capital, which helps protect it from interest rate shocks.

Business resilience: economic cycles

Resilience to economic cycles is also best supported by high returns on capital and can also be inferred from the sector the company operates in. Businesses that sell non-cyclical goods and services (such as consumer staples, low cost items and business critical services) are less exposed to commodity prices and should see consistent demand during an economic cycle. In contrast, airlines, oil companies and miners are very exposed to commodity prices. In the event of volatility in commodity markets, companies that are less exposed to commodity prices are generally better positioned to maintain stable profit margins and financial performance.

Economic downturns can result in a rise in bankruptcies. Companies that derive revenue from a large number of clients and that are not overly exposed to a single client or a handful of clients, or even to a single industry, are well-placed to weather a downturn. This is because their diversified revenue streams reduce reliance on any single source, thus spreading risk and stabilising revenue.

When analysing a company, it's particularly helpful to understand where in their customer's income statement the purchase of their product and service would sit.

- For companies selling raw materials, customers would list the expense as a Cost of Revenue.

- For companies selling services, like software, customers would list the expense as a General & Administrative expense.

- For companies selling advertising, customers would list the expense as a Sales and Marketing expense.

The reason it is important to understand this is because of the impacts of economic downturns. During a downturn a company would probably cut Sales & Marketing expenses alongside General & Administrative first, specifically discretionary spending such as marketing and travel. Next, capital expenditure would most likely be scaled back, typically by postponing new projects or expansions. R&D costs are likely to be protected at first, in order to maintain the company's future growth potential, but large R&D expenses may also be reduced or delayed. If a downturn is particularly severe, a company's response may culminate in layoffs, asset sales, debt restructuring or the company looking for a takeover bid.

The point here is to understand the likelihood of a customer ceasing its business with a company in the event of a downturn. Resilient companies are those that provide products and services that are unlikely to be cut during a downturn.

Excelling at pricing power, barriers to entry and resilience

The long-term creation of value requires a company to succeed at its relationship with its investors, supply chain and competition. The previous chapters highlighted that only certain sectors and industries are capable of producing consistently high long-term growth, high margins and high returns on capital. Such strong financial metrics are only made possible through pricing power, barriers to entry and resilience. We can now turn to the specific types of business models where such qualities are found.

Chapter 6:
Business models

Quality growth business models

Most companies don't have growth rates, profit margins and returns on capital that are consistently high, and most companies don't benefit from strong pricing power and impenetrable barriers to entry and scale. The companies that have all of these qualities, at this moment in time, are typically businesses selling software, semiconductors, payment services, credit ratings, healthcare and luxury items.

We will now consider each of these types of businesses and draw out what they have in common.

Payment companies

The credit card companies, Visa and Mastercard, are currently two of the highest quality businesses. Together they are in a duopoly and are the world's largest payment processes. There is a consistently strong demand for their service, with Visa processing over $10 trillion in transactions each year, and Mastercard doing close to $6 trillion.

Both companies have growth opportunities ahead of them. As consumer spending around the world changes and grows, Visa and Mastercard are in a position to benefit from significant long-term trends and structural changes, particularly growth in cross-border spending and the replacement of cash with digital payments.

While both have established brands recognised around the world, they have also created near-impossible to replicate payment networks consisting of thousands of financial institutions, millions of merchants and billions of card users. Establishing a competing network would require you to simultaneously convince consumers to use your card and convince merchants to accept your card, which is made all the more harder given that merchants won't accept a card that isn't carried and users won't carry a card that isn't accepted.

Networks are challenging to create as they require a critical mass of active users. Many networks struggle to attract participants and fail at becoming self-sustaining. The value of Visa and Mastercard's networks increase as more merchants and consumers use their payment systems, which in turn attracts more merchants and consumers, reinforcing their dominance. Therefore, this duopoly enjoys a formidable pricing power and barrier to entry.

Both companies are also highly resilient. The credit card companies effectively function like a toll booth for global spending. As inflation rises, so does the amount of money being spent - as a consequence of purchasing power being eroded. Visa and Mastercard take a percentage of each transaction, meaning inflation should lead to higher revenues for both companies.

Credit rating agencies

The credit rating agencies, S&P Global and Moody's, are the leading providers of credit ratings for fixed income securities, such as bonds. While they are not the only credit rating agencies, together they have the market share and 90% of the world's debt has a credit rating from either Moody's or S&P.

The business model of the credit rating agencies benefits from two types of protection. Firstly, stringent regulation provides a barrier to entry. If you want to start a credit rating agency, you will be met with a wide range of legal requirements that have to be complied with at great cost. Secondly, both S&P and Moody's benefit from switching costs. Borrowers looking for a cheaper credit rating from one of the smaller competitors will be met with increased borrowing costs in the form of a higher interest rate on their debt. This can typically be between 30 - 50 basis points higher. This means even if a competitor were to offer its services for free, borrowers would still want to buy credit ratings from Moody's and S&P, given the lower borrowing costs their ratings give access to.

Software companies

The software-as-a-service (SAAS) business model is one of the best business models around. Since 1994, the MSCI World Software index has had an annualised gross return of 13.67%, compared to 8.50% for the MSCI World. It can broadly be divided into software that is or isn't industry specific.

Software that caters to most types of businesses includes productivity software (e.g. Microsoft), payroll and accounting software (e.g. ADP and Intuit), enterprise resource planning systems for managing supply chains (e.g. SAP and Technology One) and cybersecurity (e.g. Fortinet, Palo Alto and Qualys). These solutions are versatile enough to serve the core needs of a wide range of organisations. In contrast, there are more specialist solutions tailored to specific industries. Examples include specialist software for semiconductor design (e.g. Cadence Design Systems and Synopsys), engineering software (e.g. Autodesk), architectural design software (e.g. Nemetschek) and software for life sciences (e.g. Veeva Systems).

There are four main reasons why the SAAS businesses make such good investments.

Firstly, there is minimal reliance on raw materials. SAAS companies typically do not use physical raw materials, instead their largest expense is often labour, making them asset-light and capital-light businesses. This ensures their revenue stream can benefit from wide profit margins.

Secondly, they benefit from efficient production, as their products are cost effective to replicate. Unlike the manufacturing process for physical products, which are labour and resource intensive, software can be copied and sold indefinitely without additional production cost. This makes their revenue stream highly scalable. It also allows the company, particularly for software with mass appeal, to build a highly diversified revenue stream from millions of different customers.

Thirdly, software companies typically employ a recurring revenue model through subscriptions. Software is often a low-cost investment for companies, and switching from one service provider to another can be time consuming and can create compatibility issues. Consequently, many SAAS companies enjoy high levels of client retention. Together this creates recurring revenue that is fairly predictable and fairly resilient.

Fourthly, software is protected by IP. This helps protect a company's innovation and helps create a barrier to entry as new entrants can't replicate their proprietary software and may struggle to produce something with as effective functionality.

Creating software products from the perspective of the balance sheet

A company's development of an intangible asset, like a software application, is typically capitalised on the balance sheet and therefore it is worth understanding how it impacts the balance sheet.

- Initially, cash on the asset side of the balance sheet decreases as it is used to pay for the cost of software developers, tools and infrastructure (very little is spent by way of raw materials).

- The value creation process then sees the creation of a new intangible asset (assuming that the software's development costs are capitalised). So from the balance sheet's perspective, the creation of an intangible asset (like software) is merely a transaction where cash is exchanged for the intangible asset. Instead of recording this cash outflow as an expense (which would reduce the company's earnings on the income statement), the company records it as an intangible asset on the balance sheet. The value of the intangible asset is then amortised over time.

- The company can now begin selling their software to clients, which will increase cash on the balance sheet.

Unlike physical products, which are made once and sold once, intangible products (like software, data and the digital content available on streaming services) are made once and sold multiple times - sometimes millions of times. From the balance sheet perspective, this means inventory doesn't have to go down for cash to go up. Selling the same intangible product over and over again can be a profitable business.

Defining sectors and industries

It's worth pausing briefly at this point to make a point about how sectors and industries are defined. The often used definition of a technology company is a company that sells technology. This may sound intuitive, but many companies that don't sell technology are often classified as technology companies. They may use technology and pioneer innovation in technology, but often what is being sold is entertainment (e.g. Netflix), advertising (e.g. Google and Instagram) or something else.

A wide range of companies not classified as technology companies are often heavily reliant on technology, such as manufacturers, airlines and even banks. Interestingly, a wide range of companies often classified as technology companies are actually exposed to other industries. Nemetschek is a German company that sells software to architects and engineers for use in the design and construction of buildings. Therefore, investors in Nemetschek, despite it being a software company, are exposed to the construction industry. Similarly, Cadence Design Systems and Synopsys sell software for designing microchips and therefore have significant exposure to the semiconductor industry.

Sector exposure is an important consideration when considering a company's resilience. It's therefore important to consider the underlying industries that a company is exposed to, as it is the dynamics and trends in play here that are driving the business.

Semiconductor companies

Semiconductors are the foundation of all advanced technology and advanced technology over the last few decades has been the foundation of economic growth, particularly in developed economies.

Since 2000, the MSCI World Semiconductor index has had an annualised gross return of 10.82%, compared to 6.60% for the MSCI World.

The semiconductor supply chain is probably one of the most complex supply chains in the world, particularly considering the large number of companies involved, the geographical distribution of these companies and the technologically difficulty that would need to be overcome to break through their barriers to entry. The supply chain is populated with a wide range of companies, from big tech companies like Apple and NVIDIA that design their own chips, right down to specialist niche Dutch and Japanese companies, like ASML and DISCO, who manufacture precision instruments.

Historically, companies like IBM and Intel would design and make their own chips, and would even make their own equipment for making chips. Over time, the supply chain disaggregated. The division of labour and specialisation led to many semiconductor companies becoming highly specialised, resulting in most segments of the supply chain featuring only two or three key players.

If you look at the 10 largest companies in the world, the majority either design and/or make their own semiconductors, e.g. Apple, Microsoft, NVIDIA, Alphabet, Meta Platforms, TSMC and Broadcom.

The semiconductor industry is best understood by considering:

- Who's buying semiconductors?

- Who's designing semiconductors and what tools are they using?

- Who's making semiconductors and what tools are they using?

Semiconductor buyers

Semiconductors are crucial for processing information and storing data.

Companies like Apple and Samsung need semiconductors to put in smartphones, tablets and laptops. Data centres, like Amazon Web Services, Google Cloud and Microsoft Azure, need semiconductors for their servers and data storage. Automakers, like Tesla and Toyota, need semiconductors to put in their vehicles to assist with driver assistance and vehicle management. Firms involved in manufacturing and automation need semiconductors for their machinery, robotics and control systems. Telecom companies need semiconductors for their routers and networks.

Demand for semiconductors is increasingly from a wide range of customers.

Semiconductor designers and their tools

Semiconductors can be designed and then made either by different companies or by companies that do both.

The designers of semiconductors include: NVIDIA, AMD, Apple, Qualcomm, Broadcom, Marvell, Texas Instruments, Samsung, Intel, Micron, Analog Devices and Infineon.

Companies that both design and manufacture semiconductors are known as "Integrated Device Manufacturers" (IDM), and include Texas Instruments, Qualcomm and Broadcom.

Companies that only design semiconductors (such as NVIDIA) are described as being "Fabless" as they don't have the "fabs" (short for fabrication plants) required to fabricate (or manufacture) their own semiconductors.

NVIDIA is the leading designer of graphics processing units (GPUs). While originally created for delivering high-quality graphics for gaming, NVIDIA's GPUs have become essential for artificial intelligence (AI) applications and the training of the large language models (LLMs) used in AI. Due to NVIDIA being fabless, they operate a relatively asset-light business model, which allows them to focus on design and innovations. Their software ecosystem, particularly their CUDA platform, allows developers to make the most of the full power of NVIDIA's GPUs, and has become a key competitive advantage.

Semiconductor designers need tools, specifically Electronic Design Automation (EDA) software, which they then use for circuit design, simulation and verification. The main providers of EDA tools are Cadence Design Systems, Synopsys, ANSYS and Siemens.

Semiconductor manufacturers and their tools

Once a semiconductor is designed, it can then be manufactured. There are two types of semiconductor manufacturers (or fabs): there are the IDMs (who also design their own chips), and then there are the "Foundries", who manufacture chips based on the designs of fabless companies. The foundries include TSMC, GlobalFoundries and Samsung.

Fabless	IDM	Foundries
Only design semiconductors	Design and manufacture semiconductors	Only manufacture semiconductors
Includes NVIDIA, AMD and Apple.	Includes Texas Instruments, Qualcomm and Broadcom.	Includes TSMC, GlobalFoundries and Samsung.

Semiconductor manufacturers are known for their high capital expenditure, due to significant investment being required to build and maintain their cutting edge fabs.

The semiconductor manufacturers are the largest customers of semiconductor manufacturing equipment suppliers, such as Applied Materials, ASML, Lam Research and KLA Corp.

Manufacturing semiconductors is a complex, multi-step process that begins with the production of silicon wafers. This process involves the slicing, grinding, and dicing of wafers using equipment from companies like the Japanese company DISCO Corp. Once prepared, the wafers are patterned using photolithography machines, with ASML being the leading provider. The patterned areas are then etched to create the desired circuits using equipment from Applied Materials and Lam Research. Following this, thin layers of materials are deposited onto the wafer's surface using deposition equipment from Applied Materials and Tokyo Electron. Ion implantation is performed to modify the wafer's electrical properties, and planarisation smooths the surface to prepare it for further processing. The creation of interconnections on the chip involves additional deposition and photolithography steps. Wafer testing is conducted using equipment from Advantest and Teradyne to ensure each chip's functionality before the wafers are diced into individual chips. Finally, the chips are packaged and undergo final testing, with companies like KLA Corp. providing critical inspection and yield management tools. Once these steps are completed, the finished semiconductors are ready for distribution to buyers.

ASML is often described as being one of the world's most important companies. It has a resilient business and is a vital cog in the semiconductor supply chain. ASML is the only company selling extreme ultra-violet (EUV) lithography machines, which are essential in the manufacturing process of the latest semiconductors. ASML's products are relied on and used by all major semiconductor manufacturers. For a competitor to reproduce ASML's EUV machine and create their own version, they would need a huge investment of capital, time and customer partnerships in order to source the required technological knowledge and expertise and to even come remotely close to replicating what ASML is doing. This makes their barrier to entry extremely high.

While ASML makes one type of equipment essential to the semiconductor manufacturing process, Applied Materials makes many types. It is one of the largest semiconductor companies in the world, particularly by revenue. They make and service essential equipment for the manufacturing process, which includes ensuring that yields are high. Applied Materials currently has 26,111 active patents globally. Their broad portfolio of products, from wafer fabrication to final testing, makes Applied Materials critical to semiconductor production and indispensable to the industry.

Healthcare companies

Since 1994, the MSCI World Healthcare index has had an annualised gross return of 10.95%, compared to 8.50% for the MSCI World. Several factors contribute to healthcare companies being robust compounders and frequently outperforming the wider market.

Firstly, healthcare companies provide an essential product. Unlike discretionary spending, the demand for medical therapeutics and diagnostic tools is consistently high due to good health being highly desired and valued by society. This creates consistent demand, stable revenue and sustained growth that's linked to population growth.

Secondly, healthcare companies generally have pricing power. This is the result of relatively low cost raw materials and high margins, reflecting the essential nature of the product and the complex manufacturing process required for the creation of the product. Intellectual property creates a legal barrier to entry, and trust can create long-term brand loyalty. Trust is important as when patents expire or are revoked, customers may still be willing to pay more for the quality associated with the brand.

Thirdly, healthcare companies often benefit from recurring revenue. This mostly stems from the ongoing need for medical treatment. Companies specialising in chronic disease management, particularly where medication and monitoring is lifelong, benefit from continuous long-term demand for their products.

There is a wide range of potential healthcare companies to be invested in. The MSCI World Healthcare index currently follows the performance of 135 companies. The large number reflects both the wide range of health conditions and the importance of specialisation in healthcare. Companies generally focus their expertise on specific health conditions. This specialisation can result in superior products. Specialisation creates niche markets where a company is able to obtain a dominant position.

The Danish company, Novo Nordisk, is one of the largest providers of diabetes treatments and has often had a return on capital greater than 50%. The nature of chronic diseases, like diabetes, mean that patients rely on Novo Nordisk's medication their entire lives, which creates a steady and predictable demand for their products linked to population growth. Even if Novo Nordisk saw all their patents expire, the trust that it has created with its customers is not only hard to replicate, it also means that they happily pay a premium for the quality of what's being sold to them.

The French/German company, Sartorius Stedim Biotech is one of the leading providers of biopharmaceutical tools. Their products are essential to the manufacturing of biopharmaceuticals and biologics. They sell their tools to a broad range of pharmaceutical and life science companies. Their tools often require consumables to operate and require regular servicing, which provides an additional steady revenue stream.

IDEXX Laboratories specialise in diagnostics for the veterinary market. Demand for animal care from pet owners and livestock producers is fairly constant, even during downturns. This is further fuelled by the long-term trend of increasing pet ownership and increasing demand for livestock products. This gives IDEXX a growing and resilient source of revenue, particularly as their products are primarily consumables that need frequent replacing. Their brand reputation makes IDEXX trusted by their customers, and their innovation and proprietary technology makes their products difficult for competitors to replicate.

The main high quality companies in healthcare include: AstraZeneca, Cochlear, Coloplast, Diasorin, Edwards Lifesciences,

Eli Lilly, Fisher & Paykel Healthcare, Genmab, IDEXX, Intuitive Surgical, Johnson & Johnson, Merck, Mettler Toledo, Novartis, Novo Nordisk, Pfizer, Revenio, ResMed, Sartorius, Sonova, Stryker, Thermo Fisher, Waters and Zoetis.

Luxury companies

The leading companies in the luxury goods industry are the leather goods designer Hermes and LVMH, the conglomerate owner of Christian Dior, Louis Vuitton and other leading fashion brands.

Unlike other high quality companies, for luxury companies it is their brands alone that create pricing power. There are nearly always cheaper alternatives. There are no switching costs or network effects in play, just artificial scarcity created through high prices and intentionally low supply that contributes to the perception of exclusivity.

The marketing employed by luxury companies is often counter-intuitive. They seek to maximise the ratio of people who know about their products to those who can afford to buy them. They generally do not pander to their customer's wishes and instead tell their customers what they should want. They do not increase supply to meet rising demand, as this impairs their product's scarcity, rather they employ practices that make it harder for their customers to buy their products, such as introducing waiting lists, which further contributes to increasing demand.

The brands owned by the luxury conglomerates are typically over a century old, which is a business characteristic impossible to recreate overnight.

Luxury has proven itself, perhaps surprisingly, to be somewhat resilient during a recession. LVMH reported growth during both the global financial crisis and the recent pandemic, which was significantly driven by demand for affordable luxury items. Monsoon Pabrai, of the Drew Investment Fund, explains that the reason for this is the "lipstick effect". This is where consumers during a recession still look to purchase luxury items, but at a more affordable scale, e.g. a Dior lipstick or eyeliner, rather than a more expensive item, like a coat or handbag. Therefore, the consumer seeks to spend less while still satisfying their appetite for high quality.

The main companies in the luxury space include: LVMH, Hermes, EssilorLuxottica, Kering, Moncler, Estée Lauder and L'Oreal.

The importance of both quality and growth, not quality or growth

Having considered the quantitative and qualitative elements of quality growth companies in the preceding chapters, we can now begin to draw some of the themes together.

To summarise, not all growth companies are quality growth companies.

- A company may be growing its revenue, but not its free cash flow (i.e. the company's top line is growing, but there's no bottom line growth).

- A company may be growing its free cash flow, but have low returns on capital (i.e. the company's growth is dependent on increasing amounts of debt).

- A company may be growing its free cash flow by investing at high returns on capital, but lack the pricing power, barriers to entry and resilience to ensure that growth can continue into the future (i.e. the company is highly cyclical and lacks competitive advantages).

- A company may be highly resilient, but be operating in a declining market, meaning there's uncertainty as to whether growth will continue (i.e. the company is exposed to weak market economics).

In contrast, a quality growth company grows both its revenue and its free cash flow, it consistently invests with high returns on capital and has the pricing power, resilience and the market to continue growing for years to come.

Additionally, quality growth companies benefit from a range of intangible advantages, such as:

- network effects (e.g. credit card companies),

- predictable and recurring revenues (e.g. software companies and healthcare companies),

- supply chain control - often the result of long-term and embedded relationships with suppliers and customers,

- technology that is difficult to recreate and is protected by IP (e.g. tech and healthcare companies), and

- brands that confer trust and exclusivity (e.g. tech, healthcare and luxury companies).

Such companies represent only a tiny segment of the equity market. Once an investor has identified the companies in this segment that they want to invest in, the next question they need to consider is what is a reasonable price to pay.

Chapter 7:
FCF yield
(Valuation)

Valuation

Every minute that financial markets are open, investors are bombarded with a constantly updating stream of share prices. With the value of companies frequently fluctuating, investors often ask: "how can I avoid overpaying?"

This is where valuation seeks to offer an answer.

In investing it's important to separate the company from the financial market. The previous chapters have focused on what happens inside a quality growth company. But as the shares of such companies are traded in markets where there's a multitude of other investments to choose from and a multitude of investors influencing supply and demand, it's important that we now take an external perspective to consider how financial markets value quality growth business and give them their price.

Valuation is the most divisive subject in investing. While investors often agree on whether a company is high quality or not, they rarely agree on whether a company is undervalued, fairly-valued or overvalued. This is because valuation reflects each investor's appetite for returns and risk. On top of that, it involves reaching a view on both the future of the company and the future of the economy. These are topics open to debate and where a wide range of views and opinions are often found.

The tools used in valuation

Let's start by looking at some of the main tools used in valuation.

The theory behind valuation is simple. It involves comparing the external market value of the company (i.e. the share price) with something internal to the business. This allows us to infer the valuation the market is placing on the fundamentals of the company.

The internal component can either be the company's book value (shareholder's equity from the balance sheet), its earnings (net income from the income statement) or its free cash flow. Therefore, the three main valuation multiples used by investors are:

Price-to-book ratio = Share price / Book value per share

Price-to-earnings ratio = Share price / Earnings per share

Price-to-FCF ratio = Share price / Free cash flow per share

Rearranging the above equations reveals that a company's share price growth is driven by (i) the growth of a company's fundamentals (either growth in book value, earnings or FCF), and (ii) a change in the valuation multiple (either P/B, P/E or P/FCF). The rearranged equations are as follows:

$$Share\ price = Book\ value\ per\ share * P/B\ ratio$$

$$Share\ price = Earnings\ per\ share * P/E\ ratio$$

$$Share\ price = Free\ cash\ flow\ per\ share * P/FCF\ ratio$$

The P/E ratio is the most widely used valuation multiple. If a company's share price is $100 and it makes $2 in earnings per share, then the company's P/E ratio is 50 (100/2). Another way of understanding the P/E ratio is that if earnings were to remain stagnant at $2 per share per year, then it would take 50 years for the company to earn what you paid for the shares. The lower the P/E the less time you have to wait and therefore the better value the company is. That's the theory at least. Judging a company on its multiple alone doesn't factor in its growth rate. Earnings rarely remain stagnant, particularly for the types of companies that quality growth investors seek to invest in.

For earnings and FCF, the numerator and denominator are often switched so that they are presented as valuation yields. These are still measures of valuation, but are instead expressed the other way round.

$$Earnings\ yield = Earnings\ per\ share\ /\ Share\ price$$

$$FCF\ yield = FCF\ per\ share\ /\ Share\ price$$

As already established, FCF per share is the optimal metric when considering growth as it represents the cash that belongs to us as shareholders. FCF yield is therefore the optimal metric for valuation, as it compares the cash belonging to shareholders with the cost of each share.

If FCF per share is $2 and the share price is $100, then the FCF yield is 2% ($2 / $100). Another way of understanding this is that $2 of free cash flow is generated for every $100 invested in the company's shares. Therefore, unlike the P/E ratio, now it's the lower the yield the more expensive the valuation. This is because the higher the valuation, the less free cash flow investors are being compensated with.

In the short-term, movements in share price are predominantly the result of changes in the valuation, while in the long-term, movements in share price are driven by growth in FCF.

Valuation multiples and yields represent the premium or discount that the stock market is currently offering on the company's shares. High quality companies often have expensive valuations (i.e. low yields) as the market charges a premium for being a shareholder in safe businesses benefiting from stability and predictability. Low quality businesses often have cheap valuations (i.e. high yields) as the market provides incentives and compensation for being a shareholder in risky businesses with uncertain futures.

A company whose quality is deteriorating will inevitably see investors sell their shares, which will prompt a subsequent drop in share price. A drop in the share price increases the FCF yield. This higher yield compensates new investors for taking on the risk of investing in a company that is in decline.

Valuation is therefore highly subjective as ultimately it depends on the return and risk the investor is content with. Helpfully the market is filled with a wide range of investors (from financial institutions, pension funds and sovereign wealth funds, all the way down to the average retail investor) with different time frames (from minutes to decades) and appetites for risk and returns.

The two drivers of share price growth

The most important point to take away from this chapter, and perhaps the book, is that share price is ultimately driven by growth (i.e. change in the FCF per share) and valuation (i.e. change in the FCF yield).

Growth and valuation are intrinsically linked. Taking the view that a company is overvalued means that you've concluded that the market is overly optimistic of the company's future growth. In contrast, taking the view that a company is undervalued means that you've concluded that the market is overly pessimistic of the company's future growth. If two companies have the same FCF yield, then the cheaper company is the one with the highest FCF growth rate.

To further reinforce the connection between valuation and growth, we will start by looking at how a company's growth drives its share price. For this we will need the following formulas:

$$Share\ price = FCF\ per\ share\ /\ FCF\ yield$$

$$Share\ price\ growth\ (\%) = Current\ price\ /\ Previous\ price - 1$$

$$FCF\ per\ share\ growth\ (\%) = Current\ FCF\ per\ share\ /\ Previous\ FCF$$
$$per\ share - 1$$

In the below example we model what happens when a company's FCF per share doubles from \$10 to \$20. Assuming no change in valuation (we've assumed that the FCF yield stays at 5%), then its share price also doubles from \$200 (\$10 / 0.05) to \$400 (\$20 / 0.05). This demonstrates that FCF per share growth drives share price.

	Year 0	Year 1	Growth
FCF per share	\$10.00	\$20.00	100%
FCF yield	5%	5%	0%
Share price	\$200.00	\$400.00	100%

Next let's consider this from a slightly different angle. Like the previous example, in this example the company's FCF per share doubles from \$10 to \$20, but this time its share price stays the same at \$200. Notice how now the FCF yield doubles instead, meaning that the valuation has come down. This demonstrates that not only does FCF per share growth put upward pressure on share price, it also puts downward pressure on valuation (hence the FCF yield going up). Practically this means that if you get a growing company's valuation wrong, then it's just a matter of time before growth should hopefully bail you out.

	Year 0	Year 1	Growth
FCF per share	$10.00	$20.00	100%
FCF yield	5%	10%	-50%
Share price	$200.00	$200.00	0%

Let's now see how valuation growth also drives share price growth. In this example the company's FCF yield halves from 5% to 2.5%. Assuming no growth in FCF per share, its share price doubles. As FCF yield is inversely related to share price, if FCF yield goes down, then share price goes up (and vice versa). In the below example we assume that the FCF per share stays at $10. Therefore, the share price doubles to $400 ($10 / 0.025). This demonstrates that FCF yield also drives share price and should provide a warning that not all share price growth is driven by growth in FCF per share.

	Year 0	Year 1	Growth
FCF per share	$10.00	$10.00	0%
FCF yield	5%	2.5%	100%
Share price	$200.00	$400.00	100%

Finally, let's see what happens when FCF per share doubles and FCF yield halves. In this example the share price quadruples from $200 to $800 ($20 / 0.025). Share price growth is now significantly higher than either of the previous scenarios. This demonstrates the crucial point that it's important that both growth and valuation work in your favour.

	Year 0	Year 1	Growth
FCF per share	$10.00	$20.00	100%
FCF yield	5%	2.5%	100%
Share price	$200.00	$800.00	300%

Determining what has moved share prices in the past

When you see that a company's share price has gone up over time, your first reaction should be to question whether the share price growth was driven by free cash flow growth or a change in the market's valuation. In reality it will be a combination of both, but it's important to work out which of the two was more influential. The below table sets out the FCF per share and share price growth of three quality growth companies from 2014-2024.

	FCF per share CAGR	Share price CAGR	Difference
Cadence Design	14%	32%	18%
Alphabet	20%	20%	0%
Qualys	35%	16%	-19%

Comparing share price growth to FCF per share growth reveals what has driven share price growth. For Cadence Design Systems, the difference is 18 percentage points, suggesting that share price growth has been driven significantly by the valuation becoming more expensive. For Alphabet, the difference is 0 percentage points, suggesting that share price growth has been driven nearly entirely by FCF per share growth, and not a change in valuation. And lastly for Qualys, the difference is minus 19 percentage points, suggesting that the company is now more attractively valued as share price grew a lot less than the strong FCF per share growth.

For many early stage companies, share price growth is often driven more by the change in valuation than the company's growth. While for quality growth companies, it is primarily FCF per share growth that provides the bulk of the returns, with growth in valuation also providing a welcome boost.

Growth at a reasonable price

In investing, it helps to have both growth and valuation working for you, not against you. The credit rating agency, S&P Global, maintains a GARP index, which is short for "growth at a reasonable price". This index takes the S&P 500 and selects the 150 fastest growing companies, it then selects from this sub-set the 75 companies with the most attractive valuations. From June 1995 - July 2022 the GARP index produced an annualised return of 13.01% compared to 9.85% for the S&P 500. This suggests that stocks enjoying attractive valuations coupled with strong growth have the potential to super-charge share price growth. This is often described as the "twin engines" of share price returns, where one engine is the company's FCF growth and the other is the market's valuation. Both engines must be switched on.

In their paper "Total Shareholder Return", Morgan Stanley set out the main drivers for the S&P 500's share price return. They demonstrated that from 2012-2021 an investor in the S&P 500 that reinvested dividends would have received a total annualised return of 16.6%. Of this 16.6%, earnings per share growth contributed 7.4 percentage points, a change in the P/E multiple contributed 6.9 percentage points and dividends and their reinvestment contributed only 2.3 percentage points. This again demonstrates that it is growth and valuation working together that produce the majority of share price returns.

We saw earlier that corporate finance tells us that a company's objective should be to maximise its share price. This principle extends to investors doing valuation, meaning that our objective as investors should be to maximise the value of our portfolio. As share price growth is linked to both the company's growth and its valuation, this means that optimising a portfolio for total return requires investing in companies that are growing quickly and trading at attractive valuations, creating room to grow their valuation too. Together growth and valuation can come together to deliver stellar share price returns.

Approaches to valuation

There are multiple approaches to valuation. In this chapter we will consider three techniques: (i) estimating the intrinsic valuation, (ii) forecasting the future share price and (iii) calculating the forward FCF yield.

Valuation technique 1 - Estimating the intrinsic valuation

Intrinsic valuation is a popular approach taken by investors, particularly value investors. It involves comparing what you estimate the company's intrinsic value to be with what the company's market value actually is. In practice this involves estimating a share price (or a share price range) and then comparing the estimate to the actual share price. Estimating a company's share price is subjective, as the calculation reflects an individual's personal view on various factors, in contrast comparing the estimate to the actual share price is objective, as it relates to the actual current price.

Comparing the estimate of intrinsic value with the actual market value creates three outcomes.

Shares are undervalued if: Market value < *Intrinsic value*

Shares are fairly-valued if: Market value = *Intrinsic value*

Shares are overvalued if: Market value > *Intrinsic value*

The theory is eventually the market will correct itself and therefore both undervalued and overvalued stocks should become fairly-valued. In the course of this market correction, investors in undervalued stocks should profit from the re-valuation. This investment philosophy can be summarised as: what goes down, must come up.

There are two problems with applying intrinsic valuation to quality growth investing:

1. Firstly, this approach means that low growth and low quality companies may appear to be attractive investment opportunities just because they appear to be undervalued. This ignores the prospect of long-term compounding seen with quality growth companies. Investors instead rely on the market correcting the valuation to generate returns, not the company growing. Investors reliant on market corrections require a pipeline of undervalued investment opportunities to invest in over the years, which may not be feasible in all economic environments and market conditions. They also need to be able to time the bottom of a company's share price so they can enter at the right time, and time the top of the share price so they can exit at the right time. In contrast, quality growth investing relies more on companies growing to generate returns, than market corrections. Quality growth investors are therefore content holding for the long-term and are less reliant on market timing, particularly if they decide to only sell when a quality company loses its quality. Value investing is therefore more inclined to portfolio turnover, which has tax implications as the value investing practice of selling when a company reaches what is deemed to be its fair value would trigger a tax payment on capital gains. In contrast, quality investing has less portfolio turnover and longer holding periods, meaning investments compound while tax payments on capital gains are deferred.

2. Secondly, this approach is dependent on the market actually correcting itself in order for the investor to profit from share price appreciation. The two issues here are that the market may

not correct itself (meaning the stock may stay undervalued for the long-term) or that the market may not actually need correcting (meaning it wasn't the market's valuation that was wrong, it was the estimate of the intrinsic valuation).

Valuation approach 2 - Forecasting future share prices

Rather than attempting to estimate a company's current intrinsic value, a more effective way of considering both growth and valuation at the same time, is to attempt to forecast a company's future share price. This is a two-step process: firstly forecasting future FCF per share and then forecasting its future FCF yield.

Here's a worked example. The following company has $1.00 of FCF per share, a FCF yield of 4% and therefore a share price of $25.00 ($1.00 / 0.04).

	Year 0	Year 1	Growth
FCF per share	$1.00		
FCF yield	4%		
Share price	$25.00		

To forecast the future share price we need to forecast future FCF per share and future FCF yield. We will start with two assumptions:

1. The first assumption is that the current FCF per share growth rate of 20% continues into the future. So in this instance we're forecasting that next year the company will have $1.20 of FCF per share.

2. The second assumption is that the FCF yield, which is currently 4%, will stay the same.

We can now forecast the future share price, which will be $30.00 ($1.20 / 0.04). Compared to the current share price of $25, this represents a share price growth of 20% ($30 / $25 - 1). This reflects the fact that the FCF per share growth was also 20% and that the FCF yield has stayed the same.

	Year 0	Year 1	Growth
FCF per share	$1.00	$1.20	20%
FCF yield	4%	4%	0%
Share price	$25.00	$30.00	20%

We're now going to make three modifications to our forecast to make it more comprehensive.

1. We're going to extend our time frame from 1 year to 5 years.

2. We're going to assume that the 20% growth seen in previous years will slow to 15%. So over the next 5 years this will equate to 101% FCF per share growth.

3. We're going to assume that over the next 5 years the FCF yield, currently at 4%, will revert to the benchmark, which in this scenario we're going to say will be 3% in 5 years time.

We can now estimate both the future share price and the annualised growth over the next 5 years.

	Year 0	Year 5	Growth
FCF per share	$1.00	$2.01	101%
FCF yield	4%	3%	33%
Share price	$25.00	$67.00	168%
	Annualised share price growth:		22%

You can then repeat this exercise for the other companies in your investable universe. The companies with the highest forecasted share price growth are the companies that have both the highest forecasted FCF per share growth and most attractive valuations.

The two techniques discussed so far should hopefully have highlighted two important questions that need consideration when doing valuation. Firstly, how do you accurately forecast FCF per share growth, and secondly, how do you accurately forecast the future FCF yield? As already established in the previous chapters, forecasting future FCF per share growth is tricky. A company can only grow its profits by selling more, raising prices and cutting costs. Therefore, forecasting growth requires analysis of the company's market (i.e. whether it can sell at a higher volume), its pricing power (i.e. whether it can raise prices) and its efficiency (i.e. whether it can cut costs). As FCF per share also factors in the number of shares outstanding, therefore any prediction of the future FCF per share value also requires consideration of the impact of stock-based compensation and share buybacks.

Forecasting the future FCF yield is even harder, perhaps even bordering on the impossible. This is because the FCF yield reflects the market's appetite for risk, the market expectations concerning the company and the broader economy, and market inefficiencies, all of which are highly difficult to measure and predict.

Valuation technique 3 - Calculating the forward FCF yield

The final technique we will consider is a quicker and simpler approach to ensuring that only high growth and attractively valued companies are invested in. It involves making a tweak to the calculation of FCF yield, so that current FCF per share is replaced by an estimate of the future FCF per share. This produces the "forward FCF yield":

Forward FCF yield = Forecasted FCF per share / Current share price

The above equation produces a number that reflects both future growth and current valuation. To do this practically you can take the previous 5-10 years of FCF per share values and forecast what you think FCF per share would be in 5 years time, either by using a linear or exponential regression. Depending on your optimism or pessimism about the company you can then adjust this figure to reflect expectations.

The following example takes the previous 10 years of FCF per share data for the cybersecurity company Qualys. A linear regression is then applied to forecast the value in 5 years time. In this example, linearity is 0.98, which is as close to perfect as you can find in real-world data. If we extrapolate 5 years into the future we can forecast a future FCF per share of $8.30 for 2029. For this example we will keep $8.30 as our forecast, rather than adjusting it to reflect our pessimism or optimism.

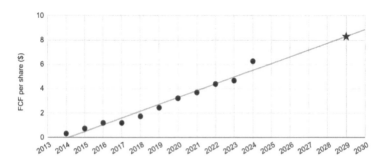

We can now use the forecasted FCF per share to calculate the 5 year forward FCF yield. Qualys at the time of writing has a share price of $153.60. The 5-year forward FCF yield is therefore 5.4% ($8.30 / $153.60). This number indicates that if you buy the company at today's price, and your forecast of future FCF per share proves to be right, then an investment today would in 5 years time yield 5.4% of free cash flow. Any share price gains would therefore be the result of the actual FCF yield in the future being less than this forward yield. This means that if the actual future FCF yield ends up being 2.7%, then the share price would have grown by 100% (5.4 / 2.7 - 1).

What makes the forward FCF yield so useful is that it allows high quality companies to be compared based on a single number that factors in both growth and valuation, without having to predict future FCF yields.

Valuation principles

Having established the dynamics behind valuation, we can now consider some important principles that should guide how we think about forecasting growth and valuation.

Valuation principle 1 - Be mindful of hidden expenses, non-recurring transactions and declining free cash flows

The measurement of free cash flow can be distorted by hidden expenses and non-recurring transactions. An example is stock-based compensation (SBC). Under the Generally accepted accounting principles (GAAP), SBC is included in the calculation of free cash flow. It is therefore important to subtract SBC where necessary, to ensure comparisons are made on a like-for-like basis, i.e. not comparing the FCF+SBC yield of one company with the FCF-SBC yield of another.

It is also important when calculating FCF to account for one off transactions. Non-recurring sales and expenses can make a company appear more or less profitable than they would normally be, and therefore can skew valuations.

Often low quality companies appear to trade at high FCF yields. However, this does not make them attractive investment opportunities. This is because FCF yield is calculated using the most recent FCF value, and is therefore backward looking. If a company's FCF is declining and the market has priced in future losses causing the share price to drop, then an FCF yield that uses the current FCF value and ignores the downward trend will appear artificially high. This misrepresents the actual yield available to shareholders. Calculating the forward FCF yield, which takes into account the future direction of FCF growth, avoids this pitfall and gives a more accurate measure of the FCF yield.

So look out for hidden expenses (like SBC), non-recurring transactions and declining free cash flows.

Valuation principle 2 - A high valuation may not mean you are overpaying

It's a fact of life that high quality is often expensive and low quality is often cheap. A high valuation does not necessarily mean you're overpaying and a low valuation does not automatically mean there's a good investment opportunity. High quality is expensive for a reason and low quality is cheap for a reason.

A company trading at an expensive valuation may have faster growth, a better quality underlying business, less exposure to economic cycles and low levels of debt on its balance sheet. A company trading at a cheap valuation may have slower growth, a shrinking market share, exposure to commodity prices and high amounts of debt on its balance sheet. Given that choice, it would make more sense for the investor to consider the company trading at the more expensive valuation. That's why investors should start by assessing the quality of a company's free cash flow, before they attempt to value it, that way they only consider good value high quality companies.

MSCI Inc. provides indices that capture companies that have high returns on capital (MSCI World Quality), high growth rates (MSCI World Growth) and cheap valuations (MSCI World Value). The following table shows that from 2014-2024 high quality and growing companies outperformed the index (MSCI World), while those trading at cheap valuations did not. This is possibly due to the value index being underweight quality growth stocks, owing to the premium that the market often charges for owning these companies. The table also sets out for each index the P/E ratio, which is a metric often used for valuation. It shows that quality and growth companies trade at higher valuations than the wider market average. As a company's quality increases, the market will price in this higher quality with a higher valuation multiple.

Index	Annualised Return (2014-2024)	P/E
MSCI World Quality	13.3%	26.2
MSCI World Growth	12.7%	32.9
MSCI World	10.4%	22.4
MSCI World Value	7.7%	16.8

Valuation principle 3 - You can buy at an expensive valuation and still make significant returns

It is tempting to conclude that a company trading at a high FCF yield is more attractive than a company trading a low FCF yield. However, it is not enough to just compare companies based on their FCF yield and invest in those with the highest number. This is because such an assumption does not factor in growth.

A company could have both a very expensive valuation (e.g. FCF yield = 1%) and a very high growth rate (e.g. FCF is growing at 25% per year). In the event that the FCF yield stays at 1% (and therefore stays expensive), next year the share price will be up 25% (and therefore match the FCF growth rate). There are numerous examples where investors could have paid expensive valuations and still made significantly high returns.

Similarly, two companies could have the same FCF yield, but different FCF growth rates. Over time, it's going to be the company with the higher growth rate whose share price outperforms. Therefore, in the instance where two companies have the same FCF yield, it is the company with the higher growth rate that represents the best value.

It's important to appreciate that growth makes valuations more attractive. The below table compares two companies. Company A is trading at an expensive valuation (FCF yield = 2%), but has a high growth rate (FCF CAGR = 20%). Company B is trading at a cheap valuation (FCF yield = 4%), but has a low growth rate (FCF CAGR = 2%). To see how this plays out, we can consider a concept called "FCF yield on cost". This is when you compare a company's current FCF per share to the share price you paid, rather than the current share price. In this instance you will see that over time Company A's FCF yield on cost is growing faster than company B's. Therefore, over time the higher growth rate leads to a more attractive valuation.

Year	Company A (FCF CAGR = 20%)	Company B (FCF CAGR = 2%)
0	2.00%	4.00%
1	2.40%	4.08%
2	2.88%	4.16%
3	3.46%	4.24%
4	4.15%	4.33%
5	4.98%	4.42%

This example demonstrates that even if you were to overpay, over time growth will bail you out. High growth stocks have a tendency to be cheaper than their FCF yield may suggest. The use of forward FCF yield, rather than just FCF yield, overcomes this issue as it factors in both growth and valuation.

Valuation principle 4 - Understand the market forces that move valuations

A company's share price is typically more volatile than its earnings. This is because share price doesn't just reflect earnings, it reflects other market forces that are also in play.

Ultimately share prices are influenced by supply and demand. There are three factors in play that impact the market's demand for a company's shares and are reflected in the company's FCF yield and therefore its valuation. They are:

1. **The market's view of the company** and whether its growth rate can continue,

2. **The market's ability to invest**, which is ultimately driven by the monetary supply controlled by central banks (i.e. interest rates and quantitative easing), and

3. **The market's view of the economy** (e.g. likelihood of a recession, high inflation, etc.).

The first factor, the market's view of the company, involves the market pricing in the company's historic earnings, the estimates of its future earnings and whether the company has any advantages over its competition that would enable it to remain profitable into the future. Share prices often jump around in response to good news and bad news concerning a company. This can include changes to management, new contracts being negotiated and signed or, for healthcare companies, results from clinical trials. At the point market moving news is published (whether good or bad), it is often too soon for the news to have made a material impact on the company's earnings and free cash flow. So the change in share price you see in response to news is just the valuation (i.e. the FCF yield) moving to reflect the market's expectations about the future.

The second factor, the market's ability to invest, is primarily the result of the activity of central banks in setting the monetary supply through interest rates, quantitative easing (QE) and quantitative tightening (QT). The monetary supply impacts equities through two routes: the cost of borrowing for companies and the cost of borrowing for investors.

With regard to the cost of borrowing for companies, lower interest rates results in lower borrowing costs for companies. This leads to a lower interest expense on existing debt and therefore an improvement in company earnings. The access to cheap finance incentivises borrowing and investment by the company into its business, which can fuel future growth.

With regard to the cost of borrowing for investors, interest rates are often described as gravity for share prices - as a low interest rate supports high valuations, while a high interest rate suppresses valuations. This is because low interest rates incentivise investors to borrow and invest into equities. Liquidity injections, seen in the form of QE, incentivise investors to become less risk averse, which prompts increased demand for riskier assets, including equities. As monetary policy is used to manage inflation, when there is a rise in inflation, not only will interest rate rises prompt a decrease in consumer spending and a slowdown in economic growth, the reduction in liquidity also makes investors more risk averse - placing a downward pressure on equity prices.

The third factor, the market's view of the economy, reflects that the wider economy ultimately impacts the future growth prospects of companies (the first factor) and the market's ability to invest (the second factor). The market's valuation of a company prices in wider economic factors such as inflation, employment, financial stability, public health and war. Changes in the earnings yield of the S&P 500 and the value of a volatility index, such as the VIX, are both useful indicators of the market's view of the economy and equities.

When companies start reporting a drop in earnings or a recession looks like it is looming, the market starts to price in the risk of a downturn. The relationship between the FCF yield and risk is positive. This means that higher FCF yields are associated with higher risk. One way of seeing this is that investors in companies with high FCF yields are demanding higher compensation for taking on higher risk. In contrast, quality companies are seen as less risky, which is reflected in their lower yields and therefore lower compensation for taking less risk.

To summarise, the monetary supply controls the money in the economy and therefore controls the market's ability to invest. Investors with money to invest need to decide which assets (e.g. bonds, equities, real estate or commodities) to allocate their capital to, which is influenced by their view on the wider economy. With regard to equities, they then need to decide which companies to invest in, which is impacted by their view on the growth prospects of the companies available to them to invest in.

Market inefficiencies

In reaching a view on what a company's valuation should be, the market considers all the available information about the company and the economy. The market then takes this information and "prices it in". This means that all known information, expectations, and projections are reflected in the share's current price and therefore the price represents the market's consensus view based on all available data. This efficient pricing in of all information requires that markets be efficient at taking in information and reaching a consensus on share price.

Occasionally prices deviate significantly from fundamentals. When the market starts to take an overly optimistic or pessimistic view of the growth of either a company or the economy, we start to see market inefficiency reflected in the FCF yield. This is known as a bubble (when prices get too high) or a crash (when prices get too low).

There are various sources of market inefficiencies.

- **Information asymmetry** - Occasionally one party to a transaction has access to better information than the other. A seller of a car, for example, will know more about the car's faults than the buyer. This same asymmetry can be seen in equity markets, which is why often investors pay attention to whether a company's management is buying or selling the company's shares. Investors with access to higher quality information should presumably be making better informed decisions than the rest of the market and therefore be less likely to misprice assets.

- **Behavioural biases** - Humans are frequently biassed subconsciously. This can lead to herd behaviour, overconfidence and loss aversion. Collectively these forces can result in share prices deviating from their intrinsic value.

- **Market frictions** - Transactions in financial markets can incur costs in the form of broker fees and taxes. These frictions can prevent investors from buying or selling assets, which can lead to mispricings.

- **Liquidity constraints** - Investors often face a trade-off between the price at which an asset can be sold and how quickly the asset can be sold. In illiquid markets, assets cannot be readily sold at their price - meaning time is required to find a buyer. Illiquidity is often seen in the small cap markets, which can create opportunities for investors looking to take advantage of these mispricings.

- **Market manipulation** - Some market participants look to artificially influence an asset's price. A "pump and dump" is when misleading or exaggerated claims are made about a stock. Once a target price is met, the manipulators sell off their holdings at the inflated price, often triggering a sharp decline in the asset's value. Similarly, a "short and distort" strategy involves talking down a stock, so that manipulative short-sellers can profit from the share price decline.

- **Economic shocks and uncertainty** - Often markets become inefficient when there is high uncertainty regarding the future. This is often seen in the lead up to recessions, during times of war and pandemics.

We can occasionally see market inefficiencies as the result of index funds and market capitalisation. Both large companies and

US companies (captured in index funds, like the S&P 500) typically trade at higher valuations compared to smaller companies and non-US companies. At the time of writing, the MSCI World Large Cap index has a P/E ratio of 22.7 and the MSCI World Mid Cap index has a P/E ratio of 20.5. This reflects the premium the market places on these companies in part due to their higher liquidity and the large number of financial institutions (particularly large index funds) that are competing to buy them. Companies that move from mid cap to large cap to often benefit from this higher premium.

When a company's shares go up or down significantly, take a look at what the market is doing. If the market is also up or down, then it's likely that the company's price just moved with the market. When the company and the market's movements aren't aligned, then the company's shares may be responding to company specific news. Given that quality growth companies are typically a lot better than the market, buying opportunities present themselves when their price is down due to the market also being down.

In light of the above, there are often opportunities for investors that result from a company's share price declining. This is because a drop in share prices does not always mean a drop in the company's quality. Rather than a deterioration in the quality of the company, a share price drop may be because the market has changed its mind on the health of the economy or because the market is being restricted in its ability to invest. These factors reflect the economy and the market, and therefore don't reflect the company being invested in. Such occasions can be beneficial to investors. Look out for buying opportunities where the share price has dropped, but the fundamentals of the business remain unchanged.

Valuation principle 5 - Understand the risk factors facing the companies you invest in

It's important that investors familiarise themselves with the risks facing the companies they invest in. These risk factors are typically disclosed by companies in their regulatory filings, such as their prospectus and annual reports (e.g. 10-K). Examples of risk factors include:

- **Market and economic risks** - this can cover the risk of economic downturns impacting consumer spending and changes in industry demand or competition. Be cautious of companies that heavily rely on a single market or region, particularly exposure to volatile markets.

- **Regulatory and legal risks** - this can cover the risk of changes to legislation, any ongoing or potential litigation and compliance with various laws and regulations. Be cautious of companies with ongoing investigations or litigations and frequent fines and investigations.

- **Operational risks** - this can cover disruptions to the supply chain, dependence on suppliers and the risk of cybersecurity threats and data breaches. Be cautious of companies with a history of disruptions to their operations and a lack of contingency planning.

- **Financial risks** - this can cover the level of debt, exposure to interest rate changes and fluctuations in revenue or profitability. Be cautious of companies with consistent financial losses, high debt-to-equity ratios and reliance on short-term financing.

- **Strategic risks** - this can cover a failure to adapt to a changing market and unsuccessful M&A. Be cautious of companies with a lack of strategic direction, frequent changes in senior management and a poor M&A track record.

- **Technology and innovation risks** - this can cover rapid technological change making current products obsolete, a failure to innovate and keep up with change and a high cost associated with R&D. Be cautious of a lack of investment in new technology and R&D, a poor track record of innovation and a reliance on outdated technology.

Valuation principle 6 - There's always something trading at a comparatively attractive valuation

Maintaining a list of the FCF yield of quality growth companies reveals that while such companies tend to have higher than average valuations, there are always companies trading at comparatively attractive valuations. The below table sets out the FCF yields, at the time of writing, of a number of quality growth companies, demonstrating that while ASML and Fair Isaac are currently trading at low yields, there are still value opportunities to be found in the form of companies like Applied Material and Automatic Data Processing. The question for investors is whether they should invest on the basis of valuation alone, or whether higher growth is to be found in lower yielding, more expensive companies.

Company	FCF yield
Applied Materials	5.00%
Automatic Data Processing	4.08%
Alphabet	3.96%
Fortinet	3.89%
Verisign	3.87%
Visa	3.50%
Constellation Software	3.35%
Mettler Toledo	3.30%
Qualys	3.26%
Lam Research	3.07%
Mastercard	2.73%
Moody's	2.64%
SPGI	2.57%
MSCI	2.56%
Microsoft	2.23%
Synopsys	2.12%

NVIDIA	1.78%
Cadence	1.68%
IDEXX	1.68%
Fair Isaac	1.28%
ASML	1.23%

Bringing it all together

In an attempt to summarise this chapter and all of the preceding chapters, the below graphic sets out how the main drivers of share price come together. Ultimately the long-term driver of share price returns is predominately growth in FCF per share, with the change in FCF yield often lending a helping hand along the way.

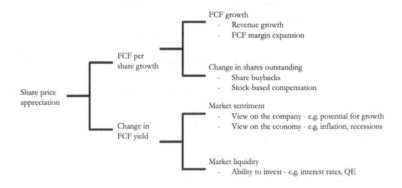

There's a lot that can be considered when trying to reach a view on a company's valuation. The following chart shows the share price of McDonald's over the last several decades. At numerous points in the company's history investors could have bought the shares and made significant returns. This demonstrates that high quality growth companies more often than not provide suitable entry points for long-term investors on a frequent basis. Quality growth companies are often undervalued by the market as it struggles to adequately price in future growth over the long-term. There is rarely a bad time to buy a compounding machine. An excellent company bought at a seemingly expensive, but not unreasonable price, and held for the long-term can still do well.

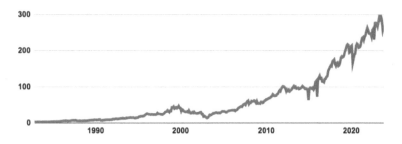

One of the most prudent approaches to valuation is cost averaging. This involves building up positions over time. The theory is that sometimes you will underpay, sometimes you will overpay, but overtime the average of what you paid should reflect the company's fair value.

In closing, investors should focus primarily on the quality of a company's business, the resilience of its cash flows and its competitive advantages. Focus first on the business and then consider whether it is trading at a reasonably attractive valuation.

Chapter 8:
Portfolio construction

Quality growth investing is more than just picking quality growth companies. Once an investor is confident that they have found a high quality company trading at an attractive price, they then need to decide how that company is going to fit into their portfolio. Should it be their largest position or should they start off small? Should they sell an investment to make room?

Imagine being forced to invest all your money and the money of your closest friends and family into your portfolio. You are only allowed to select a few investments, no more than 20, and you are forbidden from buying or selling anything for at least the next 5 years. Such circumstances would hopefully incentivise you to only invest in safe, low risk and heavily researched companies that you understand and are happy putting your money (and other peoples) into for the long-term. If these rules were in place, then the overall effect would be that you become a concentrated (i.e. holding a small number of stocks), buy-and-hold investor focused on high quality companies. If you were to take this approach, then as we will see, academic research suggests that you should actually do quite well.

What works in investing?

This next section summarises academic studies and other evidence that supports using a concentrated low-turnover investment strategy.

What works in investing? Diversified and concentrated.

One of the benefits of only investing in high quality growth companies is that your investable universe of potential stocks is quite small. At the time of writing, the S&P 500 has only 126 companies (25% of the index) with a FCF per share growth rate greater than 15%, while only 128 companies (26% of the index) have a return on capital greater than 15%. When looking for both of these characteristics, only 58 companies (12% of the index) have a high growth rate and high return on capital. The investable universe of quality growth companies is therefore quite a small segment of the wider stock market. The higher your threshold for quality and growth, the smaller your investable universe. Adding in other factors, such as high margins and balance sheet strength, shrinks the investable universe further still. This calls into question, how many companies does a quality growth portfolio need to hold? Or perhaps better put given their elusivity, how many companies can a quality growth hold?

Conventional wisdom suggests that investors should not "put all their eggs in one basket" and instead have a well-diversified portfolio across not just geographies and sectors, but also across market capitalisation, business maturity and valuation. While diversification is unequivocally important, academic findings actually suggest that diversification has limitations. We have seen that certain sectors have stronger fundamentals and better market performance than others, meaning it's likely that adding airlines and banks to your portfolio would deteriorate your portfolio's quality and compromise its long-term performance, rather than benefit it through diversification. Therefore, what you don't own is just as important as what you do own.

The 1991 paper "Investor Diversification and International Equity Markets" found that most investors are biassed towards their domestic market. US investors invest mostly in US listed companies, Japanese investors invest mostly in Japan listed companies and UK investors invest mostly in UK listed companies. Domestic investors therefore often assume that the best investment opportunities are in their domestic market. Investors would be wise to take a global approach to investing and look for the best investments available regardless of where they are listed, and to not unnecessarily rule out investments just because they are not listed on domestic markets. The lack of diversification internationally could be a potential hindrance for investors.

What a lot of investors don't appreciate is that it is possible, in certain instances, to hold a single stock portfolio and still be somewhat diversified. This is because some companies are highly diversified internally with revenues generated across multiple business lines and across multiple geographies. L'Oreal, despite being listed in France, generates only 32% of its revenue from Europe, compared to 25% from North America and 31% from Northern Asia. It also owns multiple billion dollar brands, such as Garnier, Maybelline and Vichy. This is a highly diversified business. Similarly the fashion company, LVMH, while also being a single company, owns a range of brands including Christian Dior, Moët, Givenchy, TAG Heuer and Bulgari. Likewise, consumer goods companies, such as Procter & Gamble, Unilever, Nestle, Coca-Cola, PepsiCo and Colgate-Palmolive, also have diversified revenues across multiple business lines and geographies.

The below Sankey diagrams illustrate the income statements for both Procter & Gamble and Coca Cola. For P&G it shows that the company generates a diversified revenue stream from brands operating in a range of sectors. For Coca Cola it shows that the company generates a diversified revenue stream globally. The diversification of the revenue streams of your investments is therefore an important factor when considering the overall diversification of your portfolio.

Procter & Gamble

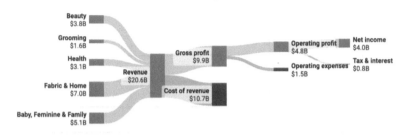

Coca Cola

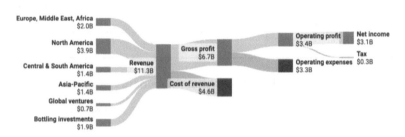

Coca Cola's income statement highlights an important point: the location of a company's listing and the location of a company's headquarters doesn't always reflect where the company is doing business. Even though Coca Cola is listed on the New York Stock Exchange and is headquartered in Atlanta, Georgia, only around one-third of its revenue is generated in North America, with around two-thirds generated overseas.

Similarly, just 71% of the S&P 500's revenues come from the US, with the rest coming internationally (a further breakdown is provided below). Therefore, you don't need to invest in a large number of companies from around the world to have a globally diversified portfolio.

Country	S&P 500's Revenue Exposure (%)
US	70.9%
China	4.3%
Japan	2.6%
UK	2.5%
Canada	2.1%
Germany	1.9%
France	1.1%
Brazil	1.0%
Other	13.6%

Academic research has shown that the benefits of diversification decay quickly. A portfolio of less than 5 stocks has a fairly significant amount of portfolio risk, while a portfolio with 20-25 equal-sized positions sees portfolio risk nearly completely eliminated, with only the wider market risk inherent to equities remaining.

It's worth pausing here to briefly discuss the wider picture of managing risk in investing. Risk can be broadly understood as taking two forms: diversifiable risk and non-diversifiable risk. Once you have sufficiently diversified your portfolio what you're left with is the non-diversifiable risk that is inherent to equity investing. This risk is best mitigated through investing in high quality companies trading at attractive valuations, where the underlying business is not exposed to exogenous factors such as competitive threats, macroeconomic events, and political and regulatory risk. Additional steps to risk mitigation can include avoiding companies lacking a track record, going through a restructuring, possessing a weak balance sheet and trading in illiquid markets.

Academic evidence supports the case for investors not being over-diversified. The 2006 research paper "Fund Managers Who Take Big Bets", found that concentrated fund managers (i.e. managers of portfolios with a low number of companies) outperformed their more diversified counterparts. The 2009 paper "Global Equity Fund Performance, Portfolio Concentration, and the Fundamental Law of Active Management" had a similar finding. They found that concentrated funds had better performance than their more broadly diversified counterparts. In addition to fund managers, the 2008 paper "Portfolio Concentration and the Performance of Individual Investors" observed the same outperformance with individual investors. The paper showed that stock investments made by households that chose to concentrate their brokerage accounts into a few stocks outperformed those made by households with more diversified accounts.

Part of the reason why concentrated investing can generate high returns is due to each investment having a meaningful size in the portfolio. If a company's share price doubles, but it only occupies a 1% position in the portfolio, then the impact of its share price appreciation would be barely noticeable. It goes without saying that the opposite is also true, hence it is important to have a balance between concentration and diversification.

The below histogram shows the spread of returns for the S&P 500 companies seen over the last 10 years. Since 2014, the S&P 500 has grown approximately 11.4% per year. Of its 500 companies, only 198 beat the S&P 500 with returns greater than 11.4% per year. Only 62 companies had annualised returns above 20%, only 14 companies had annualised returns above 30%, only 6 companies had annualised returns over 40% and only the semiconductor company NVIDIA had an annualised return over 70%. A small number of winners drive the majority of the gains. For investors this means that maintaining a greater than 30% annualised return requires you to successfully pick the 2.8% of companies that will deliver such returns, all while successfully avoiding companies that destroy significant amounts of value. Such a task would obviously require more luck than skill, but the key point from this finding is that thoughtful and selective stock picking is required.

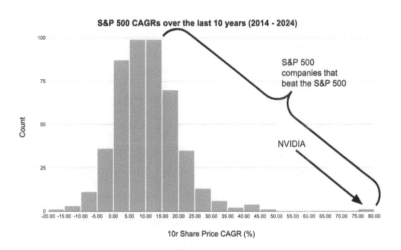

There are a number of benefits to running a concentrated investment strategy. It allows investors to conduct extensive research into the companies they own, which otherwise would not be feasible with larger portfolios. It also incentivises investors to become more sensitive to risk, as having money only in a small number of companies requires conviction regarding the quality and valuation of the portfolio.

Therefore, investors need to identify the balance between being sufficiently diversified to hedge portfolio risk and sufficiently concentrated so that a company's stock price appreciation has a meaningful impact on the rest of the portfolio. The answer most likely lies somewhere between 10 and 25 positions.

What works in investing? Low turnover.

It's worth reflecting on one of the hardest indices to outperform: the S&P 500. In order to understand how to beat the S&P 500, it's important that we first understand how the index is managed. The index tracks the 500 largest publicly traded companies in the US. The index is weighted by market capitalisation, which means the larger the company, the greater its position in the portfolio. The index only removes companies if they get too small in capitalisation and fall below the threshold of being one of the 500 largest US companies. Importantly this means that the index doesn't sell based on valuation (e.g. if a company becomes too expensive) and the index doesn't sell on position size (e.g. if a company becomes too large a part of the portfolio). The S&P 500 lets its winners run and selectively removes its losers. This has the added benefit of being a low turnover strategy that minimises transaction costs. The S&P 500 is therefore a low turnover, long-term oriented, buy-and-hold investor. These are all elements that investors could seek to replicate if they want to compete with the S&P 500.

The importance of having a long-term mindset is supported by the share price returns of companies that have outperformed over the long-term. From 1994-2024, the MSCI Quality Index returned 12.01% compared to the MSCI World Index returning just 8.52%. Despite the significant outperformance by the Quality index, over the last 14 years there have been 4 occasions when the World index outperformed it. The occasional year and years of underperformance is seen in nearly all high quality growth companies. There will inevitably always be time periods where a long-term outperformer falls out of favour with the market and underperforms its benchmark. What matters isn't short-term underperformance, but whether there can be long-term outperformance. It is therefore important to maintain a multi-decade mindset when investing in quality growth companies.

Let's take a look at what academic research says about long-term investing.

The 1998 research paper "Do Investors Trade Too Much?" analysed 10,000 brokerage accounts to compare whether the securities that investors buy outperform those they sell. Surprisingly they found that it was actually the securities that were sold that outperformed those that were bought, highlighting that investors are indeed prone to trading too much and suggesting that often the best investment decision is to do nothing.

Similar findings are reported in the 2016 paper "Patient Capital Outperformance: The Investment Skill of High Active Share Managers Who Trade Infrequently". This study showed that investors outperform when they have both active share portfolios (in that they differ significantly from their benchmark) and long holding periods (+2 years). Funds that trade frequently were demonstrated to underperform.

Likewise, the 2016 paper "Portfolio Turnover Activity and Mutual Fund Performance" compared the portfolio turnover rates of mutual funds. They found that "frequent churning of a portfolio is value destroying for investors and signals a manager's lack of skill".

To summarise, there is a strong case for being patient when it comes to compounding and perseveringly sticking to the ownership of high quality companies.

So if high portfolio turnover is bad and low turnover is good, then what about no turnover at all?

One fund has done just that. The Voya Corporate Leaders Trust Fund was launched in 1935 with one rule, "new stocks can't be purchased". The fund started with equally-weighted positions in just 30 stocks. Fast forward to today and the now 22 stock portfolio has changed significantly, mostly due to decades of M&A and spin-outs. The fund is now far from being equally-weighted, with 96% of the portfolio in its top 10 positions and its largest position, the railway company Union Pacific, now accounting for 37% of the portfolio. The fund is approximately 40% industrials, 25% energy stocks, 0% healthcare and 0% technology. It has therefore missed out entirely on benefitting from the SAAS business model and the semiconductor revolution. Not keeping up with the times hasn't been without cost for the fund. From 2014 to 2024, the Voya fund returned 103%, compared to the S&P 500's 189%. It is therefore important for portfolios to benefit from at least some turnover to keep things fresh.

Compounding and market capitalisation

Investors looking to generate high long-term returns are often persuaded by the case for investing in small and mid-capitalisation companies. The theory is simple, smaller companies have more room to grow than the largest companies. Many investors are understandably attracted to small and mid-capitalisation companies, especially given the allure of finding the next Amazon or Google while they are still small.

While the theory is sound, there are three points to bear in mind here.

Firstly, smaller companies are often in the early stages of their business lifecycle, meaning while there is scope for growth, there is often greater risk facing their business than those compared to more established and mature companies. They are often more exposed to competition and more reliant on a small number of clients.

Secondly, a company can be large and still continue to grow. In 1999, Microsoft became the world's largest company by market cap. It has since grown its share price by over 600%. In 2011, Apple became the world's largest company by market cap. It has since grown its share price by over 1500%. Being at the top of the market doesn't mean the company has reached the top of its share price.

Thirdly, and more importantly, the flaw in only investing in small companies is that significant returns in small cap investing are only generated when small companies are allowed to grow into medium and large size companies. Investors and funds focused on only investing in small caps are forced to sell their best performing stocks once they reach mid cap size, and therefore miss out on these superior returns.

The categorisation of market cap ranges changes over time due to inflation and other factors. Currently the following categorisation is generally accepted:

- **Small cap**: $300mn - $2bn

- **Mid cap**: $2bn - $10bn

- **Large cap**: $10bn - $200bn

- **Mega cap**: $200bn +

Based on the above ranges, to transition from one category to the next, a company must achieve the following market cap growth:

- **Small Cap to Mid Cap:** $1.7 billion

- **Mid Cap to Large Cap:** $8 billion

- **Large Cap to Mega Cap:** $190 billion

- **Mega Cap to greater than $3 Trillion:** $2,800 billion (note that only a few S&P 500 companies currently surpass $3 trillion in market cap)

Therefore the majority of share price returns are found at the higher end of the capitalisation spectrum. Investors looking to invest only in small and mid caps are therefore constrained by having to sell early, potentially before a company has delivered most of its gains. The agricultural equivalent would be cutting down an apple tree before it bears fruit.

It therefore makes more sense for investors to be open to all sizes. They should focus on only owning high quality growth companies for the long-term, thus allowing growing companies to keep on growing.

So what works in investing?

The evidence suggests that:

- a concentrated portfolio of

- high quality growth companies

- held for the long-term

is likely all that the average investor needs to be diversified and to outperform. This approach ensures that investments are given the time required to compound their value. The lesson here is: don't interrupt compounding unnecessarily.

Finding the best investments through scoring

Having established in the preceding chapter the four key ratios to consider when analysing a company, we can now move on to considering how to evaluate potential investments.

One approach is to have a threshold for each of the four ratios and then to score each company based on whether it meets the threshold. The following table provides a score for a subset of companies from the S&P 500. 10 year averages (2014-2024) were used to ensure that only long-term value creators and price setters were captured. For FCF return on capital, FCF margin and FCF compound annual growth rate the threshold was taken as 15%. For the linearity of the FCF growth rate, the correlation coefficient was taken as 0.85. In the table a blob has been inserted into each cell where the threshold is met. The table is sorted so that companies that score 4/4 are at the top and those that score 0/4 are at the bottom. Interestingly, the average annualised share price return over the same 10 year period for companies in the S&P 500 scoring a 4/4 was 27%, for those scoring a 3/4 the return was 17%, for those scoring a 2/4 the return was 12%, for those scoring a 1/4 the return was 10% and for those scoring 0/4 the return was 6%. So clearly there is some merit in scoring investments based on these metrics.

Company	Score	10yr avg. FCF ROC (%)	10yr avg. FCF Margin (%)	10yr FCF CAGR (%)	10yr FCF Linearity
Adobe	4	•	•	•	•
Applied Materials	4	•	•	•	•
Broadcom	4	•	•	•	•
Cadence Design	4	•	•	•	•
Fair Isaac	4	•	•	•	•
Alphabet	4	•	•	•	•
KLA Corporation	4	•	•	•	•
Lam Research	4	•	•	•	•
Meta Platforms	4	•	•	•	•
MSCI	4	•	•	•	•
Mettler Toledo	4	•	•	•	•
ServiceNow	4	•	•	•	•
Palo Alto Networks	4	•	•	•	•
Tyler Tech	4	•	•	•	•
Apple	3	•	•		•
ADP	3	•	•		•
Arista Networks	3	•	•	•	
Salesforce	3		•	•	•
Fastenal	3	•		•	•
FactSet	3	•	•		•
Home Depot	3	•		•	•

Generating investment ideas

Company	Score	10yr avg. FCF ROC (%)	10yr avg. FCF Margin (%)	10yr FCF CAGR (%)	10yr FCF Linearity
IDEXX	3	•		•	•
Intuit	3	•	•		•
Jack Henry	3	•	•		•
Mastercard	3	•	•		•
Microsoft	3	•	•		•
Nvidia	3	•	•	•	
NVR	3	•		•	•
O'Reilly Auto	3	•		•	•
Synopsys	3	•	•		•
S&P Global	3	•	•	•	
Ulta Beauty	3	•		•	•
Visa	3	•	•		•
Verisk Analytics	3	•	•		•
Verisign	3	•	•		•
Analog Devices	2		•		•
Ansys	2		•		•
Church & Dwight	2		•		•
Colgate-Palmolive	2	•	•		
CME Group	2		•		•
Cisco	2	•	•		
CoStar Group	2		•		•
Cintas	2			•	•
McDonald's	2		•		•

Company	Score	10yr avg. FCF ROC (%)	10yr avg. FCF Margin (%)	10yr FCF CAGR (%)	10yr FCF Linearity
Moody's	2	•	•		

When should an investor buy and sell?

We've seen in the preceding chapters the importance of only investing in companies that have high free cash flow per share, high returns on capital, high margins and an attractive free cash flow yield. Portfolios should therefore be constructed to maximise these four investment ratios. Consequently, any investment decision, whether it is to buy or sell, should also be to maximise these four ratios.

It's helpful to keep an eye on the lowest quality stock in your portfolio and frequently compare it to the highest quality stock on your watchlist. If switching the two cocmpanies would increase the overall quality of your portfolio, then it may be time to trade.

Compounding takes time. As long as a company remains high quality then there is unlikely to be a need to sell. Trading should be for the sole purpose of maximising the quality of your portfolio first, then valuation second.

Informed decision-making through ranking

Like scoring, informed decisions can also be made through ranking your options. The following table sets out the portfolio size, the FCF yield and the 5-year FCF CAGR of 12 companies in a portfolio (see columns 2-4). A rank has been assigned to each company for each of these three metrics (see columns 5-7). As Constellation Software is the largest position it has a portfolio rank of 1, while the smallest position, Novo Nordisk, has a portfolio rank of 12. As Fair Isaac has the lowest FCF yield it has a yield rank of 1, while Applied Material's high FCF yield means it has a yield rank of 12. As Visa has the lowest FCF growth rate it has a growth rank of 1, while NVIDIA's high FCF growth rate means it has a growth rank of 12. We can then sum up these three ranks to create a total rank. The table has been sorted by this total rank. This brings KLA Corp., Applied Materials and Fortinet to the top. These are all companies that have comparatively high FCF growth rates, attractive valuations and currently occupy small positions within the portfolio. This suggests that any allocation of capital should be made towards these companies, as this would help maximise the FCF growth rate and valuation of the portfolio as a whole. Notably, KLA Corp. didn't appear as a top position for any of the three ranks, yet it has the highest total rank overall, demonstrating the power of totalling up multiple ranks.

Holding	Portfolio Size	FCF yield	FCF CAGR	Portfolio Rank	Yield Rank	Growth Rank	Total Rank
KLA Corp.	6%	2.7%	28%	10	8	11	29
Applied Materials	7%	5.0%	25%	8	12	8	28
Fortinet	8%	3.9%	27%	6	11	10	27
Novo Nordisk	5%	2.7%	21%	12	6	6	24

Visa	7%	3.5%	12%	7	10	1	18
MSCI	7%	2.6%	18%	9	5	4	18
NVIDIA	11%	1.8%	53%	3	3	12	18
Microsoft	5%	2.2%	15%	11	4	2	17
Constellation Soft.	15%	3.3%	22%	1	9	7	17
Mastercard	9%	2.7%	15%	5	7	3	15
Fair Isaac	10%	1.3%	25%	4	1	9	14
Cadence Design	11%	1.7%	19%	2	2	5	9

How to assess the overall weighted quality of your portfolio

Having used scoring and ranking to separate the great companies from the good, we can now move on to portfolio construction. When designing a portfolio that seeks to maximise the four ratios discussed in the previous chapters, it's important to know the portfolio's weighted value of each of these metrics. For example, you may have a two stock portfolio, where Company A has a ROC of 30% and Company B has a ROC of 15%. If the composition of the portfolio were 20% Company A and 80% Company B, then the weighted ROC would be 18%. In contrast, if the composition of the portfolio were 80% Company A and 20 Company B, then the weighted ROC would be 27%. Therefore, a key part in designing a portfolio is ensuring that the highest quality companies in your portfolio have the largest position sizes.

The below table sets out how to calculate the weighted ROC of a 12 stock portfolio. For each company the portfolio size is multiplied by the ROC to give the weighted ROC, which is then summed at the bottom to give the total weighted ROC. Increasing the weighting of Novo Nordisk, the highest ROC company in the portfolio, and decreasing the weighting of Microsoft, the lowest ROC company, would boost the overall weighted ROC of the portfolio.

	Portfolio Size	ROC	Weighted ROC
Novo Nordisk	4.7%	57.4%	2.7%
NVIDIA	10.6%	49.0%	5.2%
Fortinet	8.3%	48.9%	4.1%
Fair Isaac	10.4%	45.4%	4.7%
Mastercard	9.2%	41.6%	3.8%
Constellation Soft.	14.7%	32.1%	4.7%
Cadence Design	10.7%	30.6%	3.3%
Applied Materials	6.8%	28.9%	2.0%
MSCI	6.6%	28.6%	1.9%
KLA Corp.	5.6%	28.1%	1.6%
Visa	6.8%	27.5%	1.9%
Microsoft	5.5%	19.1%	1.1%
		Total:	**36.9%**

Constructing a portfolio that is optimised for all four ratios will mean not just taking into account the ROC, but also ensuring that growth, margin and valuation are also accounted for. One approach that is quite effective in achieving this is to do a similar approach to the above, but instead of using ROC use the total rank (as per the preceding section). This would ensure that all the metrics you're seeking to optimise the portfolio for are maximised.

How to assess your portfolio's revenue diversification

Where a company is incorporated, headquartered and listed does not reflect where the company is doing business. When assessing how diversified your portfolio is, it's important to consider how well diversified the revenues are of the companies you invest in. In this context, diversification can refer to product and service diversification (e.g. Alphabet's revenue can be separated into revenue from Google search, YouTube and Google Cloud), or geographic diversification (e.g. separating revenue by continent).

A company's annual report will separate out revenue by both products/services and geographies. You can then calculate for your entire portfolio how much revenue comes from each region. Unfortunately, when it comes to geography, there isn't a global standard. Sometimes Europe is separated out by country or region, sometimes it excludes the UK and sometimes it is bundled together with the Middle East and Africa (EMEA). This can make it difficult to compare companies on a like-for-like basis. The most consistent workaround is separating North American revenue and Rest of the World revenue.

The below example is from a 12 stock portfolio. For each company the table sets out the percent of revenue derived from North America and the Rest of the World. The table is sorted by North American revenue, with Fair Isaac obtaining 85% of its revenue from North America and KLA Corp. only obtaining 12%. The right column sets out the size of each company in the portfolio.

	North America	Rest of World	Portfolio
Fair Isaac	85%	15%	9.4%
Novo Nordisk	59%	41%	8.1%
Constellation Soft.	55%	45%	9.1%
Microsoft	50%	50%	9.2%
Cadence Design	46%	54%	7.8%
MSCI	46%	54%	6.1%
NVIDIA	44%	56%	11.7%
Visa	43%	57%	7.5%
Fortinet	41%	59%	4.8%
Mastercard	33%	67%	8.4%
Applied Materials	15%	85%	10.1%
KLA Corp.	12%	88%	7.8%
Weighted avg.	44%	56%	

To calculate the weighted average, for each company simply multiply the North America column by the Portfolio column. For Fair Isaac, this gives 799 (85 * 9.4). Repeating this for the other companies gives a total of 4437, which when divided by

100 gives a percentage of 44.37%. Therefore on a portfolio basis, the weighted average revenue derived from North America is 44% and therefore 56% is derived from the rest of the world.

So despite 10 of the 12 companies in the above portfolio being US listed companies, only 44% of revenue on a weighted basis is derived from North America.

How to assess your portfolio's active share

If you want a different result to the index, then you will need a different portfolio to the index. It's therefore helpful to understand how your portfolio differs from the index.

We can compare the same portfolio used before to the composition of a relevant index. Frequently used benchmarks used by portfolio managers are the S&P 500 and the MSCI World.

The below table sets out the individual weightings of the portfolio and their respective weightings in a global equity index. While the index has a 4.53% weighting towards NVIDIA, the portfolio has a much higher position at 11.3%. This represents a difference of 6.77%, meaning the portfolio has a 6.77 percentage point higher weighting towards NVIDIA than the index. The key number in this table is found at the bottom. It is the index total of 11.79%. This means that 100% of the 12 stock portfolio corresponds to only 11.79% of the index. We can conclude from this analysis that the portfolio differs significantly from the index, given that 88.21% (100% - 11.79%) of the index isn't being invested in.

	Portfolio	Index	Diff.
NVIDIA	11.3%	4.53%	6.77%
Fair Isaac	10.2%	0.06%	10.14%
Constellation Soft.	10.2%	0.09%	10.11%
Applied Materials	9.2%	0.27%	8.93%
Microsoft	9.2%	4.64%	4.56%
Mastercard	8.5%	0.54%	7.69%
KLA Corp.	7.4%	0.16%	7.24%
Novo Nordisk	7.8%	0.65%	7.15%
Visa	7.5%	0.62%	6.88%
Cadence Design	7.0%	0.11%	6.89%
MSCI	7.0%	0.06%	6.94%
Fortinet	4.7%	0.06%	4.64%
Total:	100%	11.79%	

How to use time-weighted return (TWR) to monitor the performance of your portfolio

We're now approaching the end of the book. We've covered how to create a shortlist of potential investments, how to evaluate that shortlist based on four financial metrics and how to use scoring and ranking to inform your investment decision making. Having put together a portfolio of high quality companies, all that's left to do is to wait and monitor performance, while occasionally making tweaks to the portfolio to ensure that its weighted quality remains high.

Calculating the return of a portfolio can be difficult when there are numerous inflows and outflows of cash. You can't simply subtract the starting balance from the end balance, as your return will also include the cash that was added to the portfolio. This is where time-weighted return comes in. It allows you to account for your portfolio's inflows and outflows when calculating the growth rate of your portfolio.

An example is set out in the following table. You start the year with $10,000.

- In January your portfolio grew by 5% to $10,500.

- In February your portfolio grew again, this time by 4.8%, to $11,000.

- In March you decide to add $1,000 to your portfolio. Therefore, while you started with $11,000, your inflow means you actually started with $12,000. You also end March with $12,000, meaning your portfolio didn't grow during this month.

- In April your portfolio dropped in value to $11,000, representing a -8.3% loss.

- In May you decide to withdraw $500 from your portfolio. Therefore, while you started the month with $11,000, you actually started with $10,500. You ended May with $11,000 again, meaning that despite the cash withdrawal your portfolio grew by 4.8%.

- In June the portfolio grew from $11,000 to $12,000, meaning your portfolio grew by 9.1% over the month and by 15.2% over the first half of the year.

Month	Start ($)	Flow ($)	Actual Start ($)	End ($)	TWR	%
January	10,000	0	10,000	10,500	0.050	5.0%
February	10,500	0	10,500	11,000	0.048	4.8%
March	11,000	1,000	12,000	12,000	0.000	0.0%
April	12,000	0	12,000	11,000	-0.083	-8.3%
May	11,000	-500	10,500	11,000	0.048	4.8%
June	11,000	0	11,000	12,000	0.091	9.1%
				YTD:	0.152	15.2%

To calculate the time-weighted return for each period, you simply need to divide the End value by the Actual Start value and then subtract 1. So for January this is:

$$10,500 / 10,000 - 1 = 0.05$$

TWR is a fraction, which can then be expressed as a percentage. In this instance it's 5.0% (so multiple by 100). Having calculated the TWR for each period, we can then calculate the year to date (YTD) return. To do this we simply add 1 to each TWR value, then multiply each value, before finally subtracting 1. So in this example we simply calculate the following:

$$(0.050 + 1) * (0.048 + 1) * (0.000 + 1) * (-0.083 + 1)$$
$$* (0.048 + 1) * (0.091 + 1) - 1 = 0.152$$

Again, this fraction can be expressed as a percentage, to reveal that the year to date performance of the portfolio is 15.2%. While the time periods used in the above example are months, the same approach could be used for days or years.

You can then compare your time-weighted return to other investors or the index.

The end

Having screened and filtered a multitude of potential investments, and evaluated each investment based on their quality and valuation, it is ultimately your portfolio's time-weighted return compared to the index that matters.

Chapter 9:
Quality growth companies

Just in case you need some inspiration before putting this book down, below is a list of companies with traits consistent with being quality growth companies. Ultimately, it is up to individual investors to decide whether these companies are investable. This is not an exhaustive list and is intended for research purposes only. Hopefully, it will provide a useful starting point for your analysis. If you're interested in a frequently maintained list of quality growth companies and their quality growth metrics then visit: www.longeq.com

North America

Canada

- Alimentation Couche-Tard

- Brookfield Asset Management

- Brookfield Corp

- Canadian National Railway

- Canadian Pacific Kansas City

- Constellation Software

- Descartes Systems

- Dollarama

- TFI International

- Thomson Reuters

- Waste Connections

USA

- A O Smith

- Abbott Laboratories

- AbbVie

- Adobe

- Advanced Micro Devices (AMD)

- Agilent

- Alphabet

- Amazon

- Amphenol

- Analog Devices

- ANSYS

- Apple

- Applied Materials

- Arista Networks

- Aspen Technologies

- Automatic Data Processing

- Autozone

- Badger Meter

- Blackrock

- Broadcom

- Brown & Brown

- Cadence Design Systems

- Chemed

- Church & Dwight

- Cintas

- Coca-Cola

- Colgate-Palmolive

- Cooper Companies

- Copart

- Costar

- Costco

- Danaher

- Deere & Company

- Edwards Lifesciences

- Eli Lilly

- Equifax

- Expeditors International

- Exponent

- Factset Research

- Fastenal

- Fair Isaac

- Fortinet

- Heico

- Hershey

- Home Depot

- IDEX Corp

- IDEXX

- Illinois Tool Works

- Intercontinental Exchange

- Intuit

- Intuitive Surgical

- Jack Henry

- Johnson & Johnson

- KLA Corp

- Lam Research

- Lowes

- Manhattan Associates

- Mastercard

- McDonalds

- Mettler Toledo

- Microsoft

- Moodys

- Monolithic Power Systems

- Monster Beverage

- MSCI

- IDEX Corp

- Nasdaq

- Nike

- NVIDIA

- NVR

- Old Dominion Freight Line

- Oracle

- O'Reilly Automotive

- Parker-Hannifin

- Paychex

- Paycom

- Pepsico

- Pool Corp

- Procter & Gamble

- Qualcomm

- Qualys

- Rollins

- Roper Technologies

- S&P Global

- ServiceNow

- Sherwin-Williams

- Steris

- Synopsys

- Teledyne

- Texas Instruments

- Texas Pacific Land

- Thermo Fisher

- Tractor Supply

- TransDigm Group

- Ubiquiti

- Ulta Beauty

- UnitedHealth

- Veeva Systems

- Verisign

- Verisk

- Visa

- Waste Management

- Watsco

- WD-40

- Williams-Sonoma

- Zebra Technologies

- Zoetis

Europe

Austria

- Mayr-Melnhof Karton

Belgium

- Lotus Bakeries

- Melexis

Denmark

- cBrain

- Chemometec

- Coloplast

- DSV

- Genmab

- Novo Nordisk

- Novonesis (Novozymes)

Finland

- Kesko

- Kone

- Marimekko

- Neste

- Revenio

France

- Air Liquide

- Dassault Systemes

- Edenred

- Esker

- EssilorLuxottica

- Eurofins Scientific

- Euronext

- Hermes

- Interparfums

- Kering

- L'Oreal

- LVMH

- Pernod Ricard

- Remy Cointreau

- Robertet

- Safran

- Sanofi

- Sartorius Stedim Biotech

- Schneider Electric

Germany

- Adidas

- ATOSS Software

- Bechtle

- Carl Zeiss Meditec

- Deutsche Boerse

- Fielmann

- Mensch und Maschine

- Nemetschek

- Puma

- Rational

- SAP

- Sartorius

- Symrise

Ireland

- Accenture

- Keyword Studios

Italy

- Amplifon

- Davide Campari-Milano

- Diasorin

- Interpump

- Moncler

- Recordati

- Reply

Netherlands

- Adyen

- ASM international

- ASML

- BE Semiconductor Industries

- DSM-Firmenich

- Holland Colours

- IMCD

- Topicus

- Wolters Kluwer

Poland

- Auto Partner

- Dino Polska

- Text

Spain

- Amadeus IT

- Inditex

- Vidrala

Sweden

- Addtech

- Assa Abloy

- Atlas Copco

- BioGaia

- CellaVision

- Fortnox

- HMS Networks

- Investor AB

- Lagercrantz Group

- Lifco

- Sectra

- Teqnion

- Vitec Software Group

- Vitrolife

Switzerland

- Belimo

- Geberit

- Givaudan

- Lindt

- Logitech

- Lonza

- Nestle

- Partners Group

- Richemont

- Roche

- Schindler

- Sika

- Sonova

- Straumann

UK

- AG Barr

- Ashtead Group

- AstraZeneca

- Bioventix

- Cerillion

- Computacenter

- Croda International

- Experian

- Halma

- Judges Scientific

- LSE Group

- Reckitt Benckiser

- RELX

- Rightmove

- Sage Group

- Spirax Sarco

- Treatt

- Unilever

- YouGov

Asia-Pacific

Australia

- ASX

- Cochlear

- CSL

- Pro Medicus

- REA Group

- ResMed

- TechnologyOne

- WiseTech Global

China / Hong Kong

- ANTA Sports

- CSPC Pharmaceutical Group

- Foshan Haitian

- Hong Kong Exchanges and Clearing

- Kweichow Moutai

- Li Ning

- NetEase

- Tencent

Japan

- Advantest

- BayCurrent Consulting

- Daikin

- DISCO

- GMO Payment Gateway

- Hoya Corp

- ISID

- Japan Material

- Kao Corp

- Keyence

- Kobe Bussan

- Lasertec

- Nintendo

- Tokyo Electron

India

- Asian Paints

- Hindustan Unilever

- Honeywell Automation

- Housing Development Finance

- Infosys

- Page Industries

- Pidilite Industries

New Zealand

- Auckland International

- Fisher & Paykel Healthcare

- Mainfreight

- NZX

- Port of Tauranga

- Xero

South Korea

- Korea Ratings Corporation

- Samsung Electronics

- SK Hynix

Taiwan

- Taiwan Semiconductor Manufacturing Company